I0845367

MULTIPLY BUSINESS RESULTS WITH ARTIFICIAL INTELLIGENCE

DAVID SANDUA

"Artificial intelligence is not just a technology; it's a business mindset that is constantly looking for innovative ways to achieve more with less."

Kai-Fu Lee, Sinovation Ventures CEO.

INDEX

I. INTRODUCTION

Artificial intelligence (AI) has emerged as a powerful tool in various domains of our lives, revolutionizing industries, and transforming the way we conduct business. With its ability to analyze vast amounts of data with unparalleled speed and accuracy, AI has become an invaluable asset in enhancing productivity, improving efficiency, and maximizing profits. In today's dynamic and highly competitive business landscape, organizations are constantly exploring innovative ways to multiply their business results. Utilizing AI is one such strategy that has gained significant traction due to its potential to unlock new opportunities, drive profits, and gain a competitive edge. This essay will delve into the various ways in which businesses can leverage AI technologies to multiply their results, focusing on key areas such as customer experience, operational efficiency, and decision-making processes.

THE INCREASING USE OF AI IN BUSINESS

The increasing use of artificial intelligence (AI) in business has brought about significant changes and advancements across industries. AI refers to the development of computer systems that can perform tasks that typically require human intelligence, such as visual perception, speech recognition, decision-making, and problem-solving. Over the years, AI has evolved from being a futuristic concept to a practical tool that businesses can leverage to improve their operations and enhance overall performance. With the convergence of data availability, computational power, and algorithmic advances, AI has become increasingly accessible to businesses of all sizes, leading to its widespread adoption in various sectors. This paragraph will provide an overview of the increasing use of AI in business, highlighting its applications and the benefits it brings to organizations.

One of the primary applications of AI in business is in the realm of customer service and support. AI-powered chatbots are being deployed by companies to handle customer inquiries, provide instant support, and resolve common issues. These chatbots utilize natural language processing algorithms to decipher customer queries and respond with accurate and helpful information. They can also personalize interactions based on each customer's history and preferences, ensuring a more personalized and efficient customer service experience. By automating routine customer support tasks, AI not only reduces the burden on human agents but also enables businesses to handle a larger volume of customer inquiries simultaneously. This not only improves customer satisfaction but also helps businesses save costs and improve operational efficiency.

AI is also increasingly being used in sales and marketing to drive better business results. Machine learning algorithms can analyze vast amounts of customer and market data to identify patterns and trends, enabling businesses to target and reach out to potential customers more effectively. By leveraging AI, businesses can automate personalized marketing campaigns that deliver tailored messages and recommendations to individual customers, leading to higher conversion rates and increased sales. AI-powered predictive analytics can help businesses anticipate customer needs and preferences, enabling them to offer proactive recommendations and suggestions. This not only enhances the customer experience but also contributes to increased customer loyalty and retention. AI is revolutionizing supply chain management by streamlining operations, improving efficiency, and reducing costs. AI algorithms can analyze historical data, market trends, and demand patterns to optimize inventory levels, reducing the risk of overstocking or stockouts. These algorithms can also optimize route planning and scheduling, ensuring timely and efficient delivery of goods. AI-powered predictive analytics can identify potential disruptions in the supply chain, such as weather events or geopolitical risks, enabling businesses to take proactive measures to mitigate these risks and ensure uninterrupted operations. By leveraging AI in supply chain management, businesses can achieve significant cost savings, improve customer satisfaction through faster and more reliable deliveries, and enhance overall operational resilience.

Another significant area where AI is making an impact is in the field of human resources (HR). AI-powered tools can automate several HR processes, such as resume screening, candidate sourcing, and interview scheduling. By automating these tasks, businesses can improve the efficiency of their recruitment processes, reduce bias and human error, and ensure a more objective evaluation of candidates' qualifications. AI can also be used to improve employee engagement and performance management. For instance, sentiment analysis algorithms can analyze employee feedback and sentiments to identify potential issues and areas for improvement. This can help businesses proactively address employee concerns, boost employee morale, and create a more positive and productive work environment. AI-powered virtual assistants can provide employees with personalized training recommendations and development opportunities based on their individual needs and goals, contributing to their professional growth and development. The increasing use of AI in business is transforming industries and enabling organizations to achieve better results in various domains. From customer service to sales and marketing, supply chain management to HR, AI offers numerous benefits, including improved operational efficiency, cost reduction, enhanced customer satisfaction, and increased revenue generation. As AI technology continues to evolve and become more accessible, businesses need to embrace AI and leverage its capabilities to stay competitive in today's rapidly changing business landscape. While AI is not without its challenges, such as ethical considerations and potential job displacement, the benefits it brings to organizations outweigh the drawbacks. Businesses that integrate AI into their operations and decision-making processes are likely to gain a significant competitive advantage and thrive in the years to come.

THESIS STATEMENT

AI has the potential to greatly multiply business results by improving efficiency, optimizing decision-making, and enhancing customer experiences. One way in which AI has the potential to greatly multiply business results is by improving efficiency. AI technologies can automate routine tasks, freeing up employees' time to focus on more value-added activities. For example, AI-powered chatbots can handle customer inquiries and resolve common issues, reducing the burden on customer service representatives. In addition, AI algorithms can analyze vast amounts of data and identify patterns and trends that humans may not be able to detect, helping businesses make more informed decisions. For instance, AI can analyze sales data to determine which products or services are most popular among customers, enabling businesses to optimize their inventory and marketing strategies. AI can enhance operational efficiency by streamlining processes and identifying areas for improvement. For instance, AI can analyze production data in real-time to detect inefficiencies or quality issues, allowing businesses to take immediate corrective actions. By automating tasks, analyzing data, and improving processes, AI has the potential to significantly improve efficiency and productivity, leading to multiplied business results. Another way in which AI has the potential to multiply business results is by optimizing decision-making. Traditional decision-making processes often rely on human intuition and experience, which may be subjective and prone to biases. AI technologies, however, can analyze data objectively and make data-driven predictions and recommendations. For example, AI algorithms can analyze market trends, customer behavior, and competitor activities to identify growth opportunities or potential risks. This can help businesses make more accurate forecasts and develop effective strategies to stay ahead of the competition. AI-powered predictive analytics can help businesses anticipate customer needs and personalize their offerings accordingly. For instance, AI algorithms can analyze customer data to identify patterns and preferences, enabling businesses to tailor their marketing messages and product recommendations to individual customers. AI can enhance decision-making by simulating various scenarios and recommending the most optimal solutions. For instance, AI algorithms can analyze different pricing strategies and customer segments to determine the best pricing strategy for maximizing profits. By leveraging data and advanced analytics, AI has the potential to optimize decision-making processes and improve business outcomes. In addition to improving efficiency and optimizing decision-making, AI has the potential to greatly multiply business results by enhancing customer experiences. AI-powered technologies can provide personalized and seamless experiences to customers across various touchpoints. For instance, AI-powered recommendation systems can analyze customer preferences and behavior to provide relevant product recommendations, leading to increased sales and customer satisfaction. AI-powered virtual assistants can provide personalized assistance and support, answering customer inquiries in real-time and improving overall customer service. AI can enable businesses to offer personalized marketing messages and promotions, tailored to individual customers' needs and preferences. This can result in more targeted and effective marketing campaigns, leading to higher conversion rates and customer retention. AI can enhance the customer experience by providing faster and more accurate responses to customer inquiries. For example, AI-powered chatbots can provide instant assistance and resolve common customer issues, reducing wait times and improving overall customer satisfaction. By leveraging AI technologies, businesses can create more personalized and seamless customer experiences, leading to increased customer loyalty and ultimately multiplying business results.

AI has the potential to greatly multiply business results by improving efficiency, optimizing decision-making, and enhancing customer experiences. By automating tasks, analyzing data, and improving processes, AI can significantly improve efficiency and productivity, leading to multiplied business outcomes. By leveraging data and advanced analytics, AI can optimize decision-making processes and enable businesses to make more accurate forecasts and develop effective strategies. AI-powered technologies can provide personalized and seamless customer experiences, leading to increased customer satisfaction and loyalty. Businesses that effectively harness the power of AI have the potential to greatly multiply their results and gain a competitive advantage in the marketplace. One keyway to multiply business results with AI is by leveraging the power of virtual assistants. Virtual assistants are AI-powered software programs designed to perform tasks and interact with humans in a conversational manner. These assistants can handle a wide range of tasks, from scheduling appointments and managing calendars to providing customer service and answering inquiries. The use of virtual assistants can greatly enhance the efficiency and effectiveness of

business operations. For example, virtual assistants can automate repetitive and time-consuming tasks, freeing up employees to focus on more complex and strategic activities. Virtual
assistants are available 24/7, providing round-the-clock support
and improving customer satisfaction. By using virtual assistants,
businesses can accomplish more in less time, resulting in increased productivity and significant cost savings.

AI can revolutionize the sales and marketing efforts of businesses. AI-powered algorithms can analyze vast amounts of customer data to identify patterns and trends, enabling businesses to
better understand their target audience and make data-driven
decisions. With AI, businesses can personalize marketing campaigns and deliver targeted advertisements to specific consumer
segments, increasing the likelihood of attracting and retaining
customers. AI can help businesses optimize their pricing strategies by analyzing market conditions, competitor data, and customer behavior. By leveraging AI, businesses can set prices that
maximize revenue and profitability. AI can improve the sales
process by providing real-time recommendations and insights to
sales representatives. For instance, AI can suggest the next best
action for a sales representative based on customer preferences
and purchasing history. This can lead to more effective sales
strategies and higher close rates.

Another way in which businesses can multiply their results with
AI is by using predictive analytics. Predictive analytics uses historical data and statistical modeling techniques to forecast future outcomes or behaviors. By using AI-powered predictive
analytics, businesses can make more accurate predictions about
customer behavior, market trends, and demand, allowing them

to anticipate changes and make proactive decisions. For example, businesses can use predictive analytics to identify customers who are at high risk of churn and implement customer retention strategies before it's too late. Predictive analytics can help businesses optimize their supply chain operations by forecasting demand, minimizing inventory levels, and reducing costs. By leveraging predictive analytics, businesses can make more informed decisions, mitigate risks, and drive better outcomes.

AI can enhance the quality and efficiency of decision-making within organizations. AI-powered decision support systems can analyze complex data sets, generate insights, and provide recommendations to decision-makers. These systems can process and analyze vast amounts of data in a fraction of the time it would take a human, allowing businesses to make faster and more informed decisions. AI can help eliminate biases in decision-making by relying on objective data and algorithms. This can lead to fairer and more equitable outcomes. AI can identify potential risks and opportunities that may have been overlooked by humans, enabling businesses to make better strategic decisions. By incorporating AI into the decision-making process, businesses can improve performance, mitigate risks, and gain a competitive advantage. AI can improve the efficiency and effectiveness of business processes through automation. AI-powered robots and machines can perform physical tasks, such as manufacturing, packaging, and logistics, with precision and speed. By automating these tasks, businesses can reduce costs, eliminate errors, and increase productivity. For example, in the manufacturing industry, AI-powered robots can assemble products, inspect quality, and carry out repetitive tasks, resulting in higher production rates and improved product quality. AI can automate back-office operations, such as data entry and invoice processing, saving time and reducing administrative burdens. By embracing automation through AI, businesses can streamline their operations, achieve higher levels of efficiency, and ultimately multiply their results.

AI has the potential to multiply business results in various ways. By leveraging virtual assistants, businesses can enhance productivity and customer satisfaction. Through AI-powered algorithms and predictive analytics, businesses can optimize their sales and marketing efforts, anticipate changes, and drive better outcomes. AI-powered decision support systems can improve the quality and speed of decision-making, while automation through AI can enhance business processes. As AI continues to advance, businesses that embrace and harness its potential will have a competitive advantage and be poised for success in the future.

II. IMPROVING EFFICIENCY

Another way that AI can improve efficiency in business is through the implementation of robotic process automation (RPA). RPA is a technology that allows businesses to automate repetitive, manual tasks that are typically performed by humans. By using AI-powered software robots, companies can streamline their operations and free up employees to focus on more complex and strategic tasks. For example, in the healthcare industry, AI-powered bots can be used to automate the processing of insurance claims, freeing up medical professionals to spend more time with patients. In the financial sector, RPA can be used to automate data entry tasks, reducing the risk of errors and improving overall accuracy. The implementation of RPA not only improves efficiency but also reduces costs, as companies can save on labor expenses by automating tasks that would otherwise require human intervention. AI-powered bots can work 24/7, significantly increasing the speed at which tasks are completed. This not only allows businesses to work more efficiently but also enables them to meet the demands of a rapidly changing marketplace. By leveraging AI technology to automate routine processes, businesses can increase their productivity and ultimately multiply their results.

A. AUTOMATION OF REPETITIVE TASKS

The automation of repetitive tasks allows businesses to streamline their operations and increase efficiency. Many organizations have routine tasks that consume a significant amount of time and resources, such as data entry, file organization, or customer service inquiries. By implementing artificial intelligence systems, these mundane and repetitive tasks can be automated, saving valuable time and freeing up employees to focus on more strategic and complex tasks. For example, chatbots powered by AI can handle customer inquiries and provide immediate responses, reducing the need for human intervention and decreasing response times. AI algorithms can be used to process and analyze large volumes of data, extracting valuable insights and patterns that can inform business decisions. This not only saves time but also improves decision-making accuracy by eliminating human errors and biases. The automation of repetitive tasks through AI technology allows businesses to streamline their processes, enhance productivity, and ultimately achieve higher results.

EXAMPLES OF TASKS THAT CAN BE AUTOMATED USING AI

In addition to streamlining customer service and improving workflow processes, AI also has the potential to automate various tasks across different industries. One example of a task that can be automated using AI is data analysis. With the vast amount of data generated by businesses nowadays, analyzing and extracting insights from this data can be a time-consuming and labor-intensive process. AI-powered algorithms can be trained to analyze large datasets, identify patterns, and generate meaningful reports in a fraction of the time it would take a human analyst. For instance, in the finance industry, AI can automate the analysis of financial statements, market data, and economic indicators to provide real-time insights and predictions for investment decisions. In healthcare, AI can analyze medical records, lab results, and clinical trials to enable more accurate diagnoses and better treatment recommendations. Another task that can be automated using AI is content creation. Writing engaging and persuasive content can be a challenge for businesses, especially with the demand for personalized and high-quality content across various channels. AI-powered tools like natural language generation (NLG) can generate human-like text based on predefined rules and algorithms. This technology can be used to automate the creation of product descriptions, blog posts, social media updates, and even news articles. Companies like The Associated Press have already adopted this technology to automate the writing of financial reports, freeing up journalists to focus on more investigative and value-added tasks. AI can also automate repetitive and manual tasks that require a high level of accuracy. For example, in the manufacturing industry, AI-powered robots can be programmed to perform complex assembly tasks, reducing errors and increasing production efficiency. In the legal sector, AI algorithms can analyze legal documents, identify relevant information, and even recommend potential strategies for a case, saving lawyers countless hours of manual work. AI can automate customer support through the use of chatbots. These virtual assistants can understand and respond to customer inquiries, handle routine tasks such as processing returns or tracking orders, and even provide personalized recommendations. The 24/7 availability and quick response time of chatbots not only improve customer satisfaction but also reduce the workload on customer service agents. AI can automate the process of image and video analysis. With the rise of social media and online platforms, businesses are constantly generating and receiving vast amounts of visual content. AI-powered algorithms can automatically analyze and tag images and videos, making it easier to organize and search for specific content. This automation can be particularly useful in industries such as e-commerce and marketing, where visuals play a crucial role in attracting and engaging customers. AI can automate the process of recruitment and talent acquisition. Traditionally, hiring new employees involves reviewing countless resumes, scheduling interviews, and assessing candidates based on their skills and qualifications. AI-powered tools can automate much of this process by analyzing resumes, conducting initial screenings, and even predicting a candidate's fit for a specific role based on their past experiences and skills.

This automation not only saves time and effort but also helps to identify qualified candidates more efficiently. AI has the potential to automate a wide range of tasks across various industries. From data analysis to content creation, from customer support to image and video analysis, and from manufacturing to recruitment, AI can increase efficiency, reduce errors, and free up human resources to focus on more complex and value-added activities. As technology continues to evolve, businesses that embrace AI automation will have a competitive advantage in today's fast-paced and data-driven world.

BENEFITS OF AUTOMATION IN TERMS OF TIME AND COST SAVINGS

In addition to increased productivity and improved accuracy, automation also offers significant benefits in terms of time and cost savings. One of the primary advantages of utilizing AI-powered automation in business operations is the ability to complete tasks at a faster rate than manual efforts. AI systems are capable of processing large amounts of data in a fraction of the time it would take a human to do so. For example, when it comes to data analysis, machine learning algorithms can quickly identify patterns and extract valuable insights from massive datasets. This ability to rapidly process and analyze information enables businesses to make more informed decisions in real-time, leading to increased operational efficiency and ultimately, higher profits. Automation can greatly reduce costs associated with labor. With the integration of AI into various business functions, companies have the opportunity to streamline their workforce and allocate resources more effectively. By automating repetitive and mundane tasks, employees can focus on more strategic and value-added activities that require critical thinking and creativity. This not only enhances job satisfaction but also improves overall employee productivity. Automation eliminates the need for human intervention in certain processes, reducing the risk of errors and rework. Consequently, this can lead to significant cost savings by minimizing waste and optimizing resource allocation. Automation allows businesses to operate 24/7 without incurring additional labor costs. Unlike human employees who require rest and breaks, AI systems can work tirelessly, performing tasks round the clock. This constant availability ensures that time-sensitive operations can be carried out promptly and efficiently, irrespective of the time of day. For example, customer support chatbots powered by AI can provide instant assistance and resolve queries anytime, allowing businesses to offer seamless customer service without hiring additional staff for night shifts. This not only enhances customer satisfaction but also saves businesses from incurring the costs associated with maintaining a 24/7 workforce. Automation can also optimize the utilization of resources, resulting in cost savings. AI systems, equipped with predictive algorithms, can analyze historical data and generate accurate forecasts related to demand and supply patterns. By leveraging this information, businesses can optimize their inventory management processes. By automating the inventory replenishment process, companies can avoid stockouts and excess inventory, which can be both costly and detrimental to customer satisfaction. Automation can also help optimize the allocation of resources by ensuring that the right resources are allocated to the right tasks at the right time. For example, AI-powered scheduling software can efficiently manage employee shifts and allocate resources based on demand fluctuations, resulting in efficient resource utilization and cost savings.

Automation can significantly reduce the time and effort required for data entry and data management tasks. AI-powered tools and software can parse, categorize, and organize data quickly and accurately. This eliminates the need for manual data entry and reduces the chances of errors associated with human data processing. By automating data management processes, businesses can have access to up-to-date and accurate information, which plays a crucial role in making informed decisions. Automation can also aid in data analysis by providing advanced analytics capabilities. AI systems can identify trends, patterns, and anomalies in data that humans may not be able to detect. This can enable businesses to gain valuable insights that can drive strategic decision-making and enhance overall performance.

The benefits of automation in terms of time and cost savings are significant for businesses. By leveraging AI-powered automation, companies can complete tasks faster, reduce labor costs, operate round the clock, optimize resource utilization, and streamline data management processes. These benefits translate into increased operational efficiency, improved accuracy, higher productivity, and ultimately, enhanced profitability. As AI continues to advance, its role in driving business success is likely to become even more pivotal, making it essential for businesses to embrace automation to stay competitive in today's rapidly evolving marketplace.

B. STREAMLINING OPERATIONS THROUGH PREDICTIVE ANALYTICS

Another way businesses can multiply their results is through streamlining operations with the help of predictive analytics. Predictive analytics leverages historical and real-time data to forecast future outcomes and trends. By utilizing this technique, companies can make more informed decisions and optimize their operations for maximum efficiency. One of the key areas where predictive analytics can be applied is in demand forecasting. By analyzing past sales data and market trends, businesses can accurately predict future customer demand and plan their production and inventory accordingly. This prevents overproduction or understocking, both of which can result in unnecessary costs and lost sales opportunities. Predictive analytics can also be used to improve supply chain management. By analyzing data related to suppliers, logistics, and other factors, companies can identify potential bottlenecks or inefficiencies in their supply chain and take proactive measures to mitigate them. This ensures a smooth flow of goods from suppliers to customers, reducing lead times and increasing customer satisfaction. The application of predictive analytics is not limited to demand forecasting and supply chain management; it can also be used in various other areas such as pricing optimization, resource allocation, and risk management. For instance, by analyzing customer behavior and market conditions, businesses can set optimal prices for their products or services to maximize revenue. Predictive analytics can also help in determining the most efficient way to allocate resources across different departments or projects, ensuring that they are utilized in the most productive manner. It can aid in identifying potential risks or frauds by detecting patterns or anomalies in data that might indicate fraudulent activities. By streamlining operations through predictive analytics, businesses can achieve significant cost savings, improved customer satisfaction, and increased competitiveness in the market.

UTILIZATION OF AI ALGORITHMS TO FORECAST DEMAND AND OPTIMIZE SUPPLY CHAIN

The utilization of AI algorithms to forecast demand and optimize the supply chain is another powerful way to multiply business results. In today's fast-paced and globally connected world, businesses are constantly striving to meet customer demands efficiently and effectively. Accurately forecasting demand and managing the supply chain can be complex and challenging. By harnessing the power of AI algorithms, businesses can enhance their forecasting abilities and optimize their supply chains, leading to improved customer satisfaction and higher profitability.

AI algorithms can analyze vast amounts of data from various sources, including historical sales data, market trends, social media sentiment, and economic indicators, to forecast demand accurately. Traditional demand forecasting methods often rely on historical trends and intuition, which can be limited in their accuracy. AI algorithms can analyze complex patterns and correlations in large datasets to identify hidden insights and predict future demand more accurately. With advanced predictive analytics, businesses can proactively adjust their production and inventory levels to meet anticipated demand. By leveraging AI algorithms, companies can avoid overstocking, which can lead to costly inventory holding and obsolescence, as well as understocking, which results in lost sales and dissatisfied customers. AI algorithms can provide real-time demand forecasts, enabling businesses to rapidly respond to changing customer preferences and market conditions. Optimizing the supply chain is crucial for businesses to reduce costs, improve operational efficiency, and deliver products to customers in a timely manner. AI algorithms can analyze various factors, such as supplier performance, transportation costs, production capacity, and inventory levels, to identify the most efficient and cost-effective supply chain configurations. By minimizing inventory holding costs and transportation expenses, businesses can allocate their resources more effectively and maximize their profitability.

AI algorithms can also leverage real-time data from sensors, RFID tags, and other IoT devices to monitor and track the movement of goods throughout the supply chain. This enables businesses to identify bottlenecks, optimize routing, and reduce lead times. For example, AI algorithms can use real-time data on traffic conditions and weather patterns to optimize route planning and minimize delivery delays. AI algorithms can enable businesses to evaluate and select the most suitable suppliers and partners based on various criteria, such as price, quality, reliability, and sustainability. By automating the supplier selection process, businesses can save time and resources, as well as ensure that they collaborate with trusted and dependable partners. In addition to forecasting demand and optimizing the supply chain, AI algorithms can also enable businesses to personalize their offerings and enhance the customer experience. By analyzing vast amounts of customer data, including preferences, purchasing behavior, and browsing history, AI algorithms can identify individual customer needs and recommend personalized products or services. This not only increases customer satisfaction but also improves business revenues through cross-selling and upselling opportunities. AI algorithms can facilitate dynamic pricing, allowing businesses to adjust prices in real-time based on factors such as demand, competition, and customer willingness to pay. By leveraging AI algorithms, businesses can optimize their pricing strategies to maximize profitability while remaining competitive in the market. The utilization of AI algorithms to forecast demand and optimize the supply chain holds immense potential for businesses to multiply their results. By accurately predicting demand, businesses can avoid unnecessary inventory costs and satisfy customer expectations more effectively. Optimizing the supply chain through AI algorithms enables businesses to reduce costs, improve operational efficiency, and ensure timely delivery to customers. AI algorithms can personalize offerings, enhance the customer experience, and enable dynamic pricing, further driving business growth and profitability. As businesses continue to embrace AI technologies, those that harness the power of AI algorithms in demand forecasting and supply chain optimization will gain a competitive edge in the market and achieve exponential business results.

BENEFITS OF PREDICTIVE ANALYTICS IN REDUCING WASTE AND IMPROVING INVENTORY MANAGEMENT

Another significant benefit of predictive analytics is its ability to reduce waste and improve inventory management. By analyzing historical data, market trends, and customer behavior patterns, businesses can accurately forecast demand for their products or services. This forecasting capability enables companies to optimize their inventory levels, ensuring that they neither run out of stock nor carry excessive inventory. With better inventory management, businesses can reduce waste by minimizing overstocking and the need for expensive stockouts or write-offs. According to a study conducted by the Retail Systems Research (RSR), companies that successfully utilize predictive analytics in their inventory management processes experience a 22% reduction in out-of-stock inventory. Predictive analytics can also help identify slow-moving products or items nearing expiration, allowing businesses to take proactive measures, such as discounts or targeted marketing campaigns, to sell these items before they become obsolete. This proactive approach not only prevents wastage but also boosts overall profitability. In fact, a study by Gartner found that organizations leveraging predictive analytics achieve a 15% increase in profitability. This improvement in inventory management through predictive analytics not only saves money but also improves customer satisfaction by ensuring the availability of products when and where they are needed. This, in turn, can lead to increased customer loyalty and positive word-of-mouth, which is crucial in today's competitive business landscape. Leveraging the power of predictive analytics in inventory management can have a significant impact on a company's bottom line and operational efficiency, making it an imperative for businesses in their quest to multiply their results with AI.

C. ENHANCING PRODUCTIVITY THROUGH AI-POWERED TOOLS AND APPLICATIONS

In addition to streamlining business processes, AI-powered tools and applications have the potential to greatly enhance productivity in various domains. One such area where AI can be leveraged is in customer service and support. AI-powered chatbots are revolutionizing customer interactions by providing prompt and personalized responses to inquiries and resolving issues efficiently. These chatbots are capable of quickly analyzing customer queries and providing relevant information or assistance. By reducing the waiting time for customers and ensuring consistent availability, AI-powered chatbots enhance customer satisfaction and enable businesses to handle large volumes of customer interactions simultaneously. AI can be used to automate repetitive and mundane tasks, allowing employees to focus on more complex and value-added activities. For instance, data entry and analysis can be automated using AI algorithms, saving time and effort for employees involved in handling large datasets. Similarly, in the healthcare sector, AI-powered tools can help with streamlining diagnostic processes and support medical professionals in making accurate and timely decisions. By analyzing vast amounts of patient data and medical records, AI algorithms can identify patterns and help physicians in diagnosing diseases and suggesting appropriate treatments. In this way, AI tools enhance both the efficiency and effectiveness of healthcare services, ultimately leading to improved patient outcomes. AI-powered tools are facilitating advancements in research and development by accelerating data analysis and decision-making processes. For instance, in drug discovery, AI algorithms can efficiently analyze large chemical and biological datasets to identify potential drug candidates, significantly reducing the time and cost involved in developing new pharmaceuticals. Similarly, in the field of materials science, AI-powered tools can aid in predicting and designing new materials with desired properties, contributing to innovations in various industries such as electronics, aerospace, and renewable energy. AI can enhance productivity in the realm of marketing and advertising. AI-powered tools can analyze vast amounts of customer data to identify trends, preferences, and purchase patterns, enabling businesses to tailor their marketing strategies accordingly. By delivering personalized advertisements and recommendations to customers, businesses can significantly improve their marketing ROI and increase conversion rates. AI-powered tools can also automate the process of creating and optimizing advertising campaigns, saving time and effort for marketers. This allows them to focus on strategic planning and creative tasks, thereby enhancing productivity and effectiveness in marketing activities. AI-powered tools and applications are transforming the education sector by enabling personalized and adaptive learning experiences. AI algorithms can analyze students' performance and learning preferences to provide tailored recommendations and feedback, enhancing their learning outcomes. AI chatbots can assist students with homework, answer questions, and facilitate discussions, providing an additional resource for learning outside the classroom. AI can streamline administrative tasks in educational institutions, such as grading assignments and managing student records, thereby freeing up valuable time for teachers to focus on teaching and student support. AI-powered tools and applications are revolutionizing various aspects of business and society, enhancing productivity, efficiency, and innovation. From customer service and support to healthcare, research and development, marketing and advertising, and education, AI is transforming numerous domains by automating tasks, analyzing vast amounts of data, and enhancing decision-making capabilities. Businesses and institutions that embrace AI and leverage its potential stand to gain a competitive advantage in today's fast-paced and data-driven world. While AI is not without its challenges and considerations, its transformative power in enhancing productivity and multiplying business results cannot be overlooked.

EXAMPLES OF AI TOOLS THAT CAN IMPROVE PRODUCTIVITY ACROSS DIFFERENT BUSINESS FUNCTIONS

In addition to streamlining customer service and boosting sales, AI tools have the potential to greatly improve productivity across various business functions. One such example is the implementation of chatbots in human resources. Traditionally, HR departments spent a significant amount of time handling routine employee inquiries, such as questions about vacation days, benefits, or the status of a job application. By leveraging AI-powered chatbots, HR professionals can automate these tasks, freeing up their time to focus on more strategic initiatives. These chatbots are designed to understand natural language and provide accurate responses, allowing employees to quickly obtain the information they need. AI tools can be employed in the recruitment process to assist with resume screening and initial candidate evaluations. This not only saves time but also reduces bias in the hiring process, ensuring a fair and effective selection of candidates. AI tools can be utilized in finance and accounting departments to improve productivity. For instance, machine learning algorithms can automate the process of data entry, reconciliation, or even detecting anomalies in financial statements, thus reducing human error and increasing efficiency. AI-powered predictive analytics can deliver valuable insights for financial forecasting and risk assessment, aiding decision-making processes. This enables finance professionals to allocate their time and resources more efficiently, focusing on strategic financial planning rather than mundane tasks. AI tools can be applied in supply chain management to optimize inventory planning and reduce logistical inefficiencies. By analyzing historical data, AI algorithms can predict demand patterns accurately, allowing businesses to maintain optimal levels of stock and avoid stockouts or overstocking situations. AI tools can improve transportation route planning, considering factors such as traffic conditions, weather, and fuel efficiency, resulting in reduced delivery times and costs. AI-powered recommendation systems can be employed in marketing functions to enhance customer engagement. For instance, by analyzing customer preferences and behaviors, AI algorithms can generate personalized product recommendations, ensuring a tailored user experience. AI tools can automatically segment customers based on their demographics, buying habits, or responses to marketing campaigns, enabling marketers to target specific customer groups and allocate their resources effectively. AI-powered sentiment analysis can monitor social media platforms to gauge customer sentiment towards a brand or a product, allowing marketers to adapt their strategies accordingly. Another area where AI can improve productivity is in the field of project management. By leveraging AI tools, project managers can automate repetitive tasks, such as scheduling, resource allocation, or progress tracking. This not only saves time but also reduces the risk of human error. AI algorithms can analyze project data to provide insights into potential bottlenecks or areas of improvement, enabling project managers to make data-driven decisions. AI tools can enhance collaboration within project teams by providing real-time communication and document sharing capabilities, thus enabling seamless collaboration across different locations and time zones. AI tools can be leveraged by legal departments to improve productivity. For example, AI-powered software can review and analyze legal contracts, identifying potential risks, deviations from standard terms, or missing clauses. This reduces the time and effort required by legal professionals to manually review contracts, allowing them to focus on higher-value tasks. AI-powered predictive analytics can assess the probability of success in legal cases, aiding decision-making processes. AI tools can assist in legal research, automatically curating and analyzing vast amounts of legal documentation to provide relevant information for legal professionals. AI tools have the potential to revolutionize various business functions and significantly improve productivity. Whether it is through the utilization of chatbots in human resources, automation in finance and accounting, optimization in supply chain management, personalization in marketing, streamlining project management, or enhancing efficiency in legal departments, AI can augment the capabilities of professionals and enable them to focus on more strategic and value-adding tasks. As technology continues to advance, businesses that harness the power of AI tools are likely to gain a competitive edge in today's rapidly evolving marketplace.

BENEFITS OF USING AI TOOLS IN TERMS OF INCREASED EFFICIENCY AND ACCURACY

The use of AI tools offers significant benefits in terms of increased efficiency and accuracy. AI technologies are designed to perform tasks with a higher level of precision and speed than humans, resulting in improved overall efficiency. For instance, in the field of customer service, AI-powered chatbots can provide real-time responses to customer queries, assisting in addressing their concerns promptly. This not only saves time but also ensures customer satisfaction by providing quick and accurate solutions. AI tools can handle large amounts of data quickly and accurately, allowing businesses to process and analyze information more efficiently. For example, AI algorithms can analyze sales data to identify patterns and trends, enabling businesses to make informed decisions regarding inventory management and marketing strategies. This not only saves time but can also lead to cost savings and increased profitability. In the healthcare industry, AI tools can enhance accuracy by assisting in the diagnosis of diseases. AI algorithms can analyze medical images such as X-rays and MRIs, helping doctors detect abnormalities with greater precision and reducing the chances of misdiagnosis. This can lead to more effective treatments and improved patient outcomes. AI tools can automate repetitive tasks, freeing up human resources to focus on more complex and strategic activities. For example, in the field of accounting, AI-powered software can automate data entry and invoice processing, eliminating the need for manual labor and reducing the chances of human error. This not only saves time but also increases accuracy and reduces the risk of financial discrepancies. AI tools can assist in streamlining workflows by identifying bottlenecks and suggesting optimization strategies. By analyzing data and patterns, AI algorithms can identify areas that require improvement and propose solutions to enhance efficiency. This can help businesses identify areas of improvement and make informed decisions to streamline operations and maximize productivity. AI tools can provide personalized experiences to customers, further enhancing efficiency. By analyzing customer data and preferences, AI algorithms can offer tailored recommendations and suggestions, improving the customer experience and increasing the likelihood of repeat business. For instance, e-commerce platforms can use AI-powered recommendation engines to suggest products based on a customer's browsing history and preferences, increasing the chances of a purchase. This not only improves efficiency by reducing the time spent searching for desired products but also enhances customer satisfaction by providing personalized recommendations. The use of AI tools offers significant benefits in terms of increased efficiency and accuracy. These technologies are capable of performing tasks with precision and speed, saving time and ensuring accurate results. From customer service to data analysis, AI tools can handle large amounts of data quickly and accurately, leading to more efficient decision-making and cost savings. In various industries, such as healthcare and accounting, AI tools can enhance accuracy by assisting in the diagnosis of diseases and automating repetitive tasks. AI tools can streamline workflows by identifying bottle-

necks and suggesting optimization strategies, leading to improved efficiency and increased productivity. AI tools can provide
personalized experiences to customers, improving the overall
customer experience and increasing the likelihood of repeat business. With these benefits, businesses can leverage AI tools to
multiply their results and gain a competitive edge in today's
fast-paced and data-driven world. One of the most significant
ways to multiply business results with AI is through enhanced
customer experience. AI technologies have the capability to
analyze vast amounts of data and provide personalized recommendations and solutions to individual customers. This level of
personalization creates a seamless and engaging customer journey, leading to increased customer satisfaction and loyalty. For
instance, companies can leverage AI-powered chatbots to provide 24/7 customer support, ensuring timely and accurate responses to customer inquiries. These chatbots can handle basic
customer queries, freeing up human customer service representatives to focus on more complex issues. AI can be used to
create virtual shopping assistants that tailor product recommendations based on individual customer preferences and purchase
history. This not only streamlines the shopping process but also
increases the likelihood of repeat purchases and upselling opportunities. AI can significantly improve the efficiency and effectiveness of marketing and advertising campaigns. Traditional
marketing strategies often rely on manual analysis and intuition.
With the power of AI, businesses can gain valuable insights into
consumer behavior and preferences, enabling them to optimize
their marketing efforts. AI algorithms can analyze large volumes
of customer data, such as browsing history, social media acti-

vity, and purchase patterns, to develop a comprehensive understanding of individual customers. This information can then be used to deliver targeted and relevant marketing campaigns. For example, AI can segment customers based on their preferences and create personalized email campaigns or social media advertisements tailored to each group. This targeted approach not only increases the likelihood of customer engagement but also improves the return on investment for marketing initiatives. In addition to customer experience and marketing, AI can also be applied to various operational aspects of a business, leading to increased efficiency and cost savings. AI-powered automation can streamline repetitive and time-consuming tasks, freeing up employees to focus on higher-value activities. For instance, AI can automate data entry and processing tasks, reducing the risk of human error and increasing operational efficiency. AI can be utilized to optimize inventory management and supply chain operations. By analyzing historical data, real-time market demand, and external factors such as weather conditions or economic trends, AI algorithms can accurately forecast demand and recommend optimal inventory levels. This can help businesses avoid overstocking or understocking, reducing costs associated with inventory management. Another area where AI can have a significant impact is in risk assessment and fraud detection. By analyzing vast amounts of data, AI algorithms can identify patterns and anomalies that may indicate fraudulent activities. This can help businesses to detect and prevent fraudulent transactions, reducing financial losses and protecting their reputation. AI can also be used to assess risks associated with various business decisions, such as investments or partnerships. By analyzing historical data and market trends, AI can provide insights and recommendations to guide decision-making processes, minimizing risks and maximizing opportunities.

AI can also facilitate data-driven decision-making processes by providing insights and recommendations based on data analysis. Through predictive analytics, AI algorithms can analyze historical data and identify trends or patterns that can inform decision-making. For example, AI can analyze sales data and market trends to predict future demand, helping businesses make informed decisions regarding production and inventory levels. AI can also be used to optimize pricing strategies by analyzing customer behavior and market dynamics. This can help businesses maximize revenue and profits by dynamically adjusting prices based on demand elasticity. There are numerous ways in which AI can multiply business results. Enhanced customer experience, improved marketing and advertising campaigns, operational efficiency, risk assessment and fraud detection, and data-driven decision-making are just a few examples of how AI can drive business growth and success. As businesses continue to adopt and integrate AI technologies into their operations, they will undoubtedly unlock new opportunities to improve performance, increase competitiveness, and achieve sustainable growth. Embracing AI as a strategic tool is crucial for businesses to stay ahead in today's rapidly evolving marketplace.

III. OPTIMIZING DECISION-MAKING

In today's fast-paced and competitive business environment, making effective decisions is crucial for the success and growth of an organization. With the advancements in artificial intelligence (AI) technology, businesses now have access to a powerful tool that can optimize decision-making processes. AI can assist decision-makers by providing them with valuable insights, automating routine tasks, and enabling data-driven decision-making. One way AI can optimize decision-making is by providing decision-makers with valuable insights. AI algorithms can analyze vast amounts of data and extract meaningful patterns and trends that might otherwise go unnoticed. This enables decision-makers to make informed decisions based on real-time and accurate information. For example, AI can analyze customer data to identify trends and preferences, allowing businesses to tailor their marketing strategies and offerings accordingly. By leveraging AI-generated insights, decision-makers can make more strategic and targeted decisions, leading to improved business outcomes. Another way AI can optimize decision-making is by automating routine and repetitive tasks. Many decisions in business involve mundane tasks that can be time-consuming and prone to errors. By automating these tasks through AI technologies, decision-makers can save valuable time and resources, allowing them to focus on more strategic and value-added activities. For instance, AI-powered chatbots can handle customer inquiries and provide personalized recommendations, reducing the need for human intervention and streamlining the decision-making process. By automating routine tasks, AI enables decision-makers to allocate their time and energy to critical decision-making tasks, ultimately enhancing business productivity and efficiency. AI enables data-driven decision-making, which can significantly optimize decision-making processes. In today's data-driven economy, organizations collect and generate massive amounts of data every day. AI technologies can process and analyze this data, providing decision-makers with valuable insights and actionable recommendations. By leveraging AI, decision-makers can base their decisions on factual and evidence-based information, rather than relying on intuition or personal biases. This data-driven approach enhances the accuracy and reliability of decision-making, leading to better outcomes and minimizing the risks associated with subjective decision-making. AI can optimize decision-making by enabling predictive modeling and scenario planning. AI algorithms can analyze historical data and identify patterns and correlations that can be used to make predictions about future scenarios. Decision-makers can use these predictive models to assess the potential impact of their decisions and evaluate different scenarios before implementing them. This allows decision-makers to anticipate risks, evaluate potential outcomes, and make more informed decisions. For example, AI algorithms can predict customer demand, enabling businesses to optimize their inventory levels and improve supply chain management. By enabling predictive modeling and scenario planning, AI empowers decision-makers to make proactive rather than reactive decisions, enhancing business agility and resilience. AI can optimize decision-making by facilitating collaborative decision-making processes. With the rise of remote work and global organizations, decision-making processes have become more complex and dispersed. AI technologies can bridge the gap between decision-makers by providing real-time collaboration and communication platforms. Decision-makers can access and analyze data, exchange ideas, and reach consensus more efficiently, regardless of their physical location. By facilitating collaborative decision-making, AI promotes transparency, inclusivity, and collective intelligence, leading to better decision outcomes and fostering a culture of collaboration within organizations. AI technologies offer significant potential for optimizing decision-making processes in businesses. By providing valuable insights, automating routine tasks, enabling data-driven decision-making, facilitating predictive modeling and scenario planning, and supporting collaborative decision-making, AI empowers decision-makers to make more informed, accurate, and strategic decisions. As businesses strive to remain competitive and agile in an ever-changing landscape, harnessing the power of AI to optimize decision-making processes is becoming increasingly critical. By leveraging AI technologies effectively, businesses can multiply their results and drive sustainable growth in the digital era.

A. LEVERAGING AI FOR DATA-DRIVEN DECISION-MAKING

By leveraging AI for data-driven decision-making, businesses can experience a multitude of benefits that ultimately lead to amplified results. One significant advantage is the ability to extract valuable insights from vast amounts of data. AI technology has the capability to process and analyze large datasets quickly and efficiently, uncovering patterns and trends that may not be apparent to human analysts. This allows businesses to make more informed decisions, as they can base their strategies on evidence rather than gut feelings. AI can assist in identifying correlations and causal relationships that might have otherwise gone unnoticed, enabling businesses to implement targeted interventions and optimizations. For example, an e-commerce company could leverage AI to analyze customer browsing and purchase behavior, identifying which products are frequently bought together. This information could then be used to optimize product recommendations, tailoring them to individual customers and ultimately increasing sales. Another benefit of leveraging AI for data-driven decision-making is the ability to automate decision-making processes. By training AI models on historical data and customer feedback, businesses can develop algorithms that make intelligent decisions with minimal human intervention. This not only saves time and resources but also ensures consistency and reduces the possibility of human error. For instance, a manufacturing company could train an AI model to identify potential defects in products based on image analysis. This would enable the company to automate the quality control process, significantly reducing the need for manual inspections and improving overall product quality. AI has the potential to enhance the speed and accuracy of decision-making. Traditional decision-making processes can be time-consuming, as they often require extensive research, analysis, and deliberation. AI-powered analytics tools can efficiently process vast amounts of data and generate insights in real-time. This enables businesses to quickly adapt to changing market conditions and make timely decisions that can give them a competitive edge. For instance, a financial institution could leverage AI to analyze market trends and customer data, enabling them to make real-time trading decisions and capitalize on profitable opportunities. Leveraging AI for data-driven decision-making can lead to enhanced innovation and creativity. By analyzing large datasets and uncovering hidden insights, AI can provide businesses with a fresh perspective that can spur new ideas and solutions. This is particularly valuable in industries that require continuous innovation and adaptation. For example, an advertising agency could leverage AI to analyze consumer sentiment and preferences, helping them develop more effective and engaging marketing campaigns. The insights provided by AI can assist businesses in identifying untapped opportunities, understanding customer needs, and developing innovative products and services. Leveraging AI for data-driven decision-making provides businesses with a wide array of benefits that serve to multiply their results. From extracting valuable insights from large datasets to automating decision-making processes, AI offers a multitude of advantages that can greatly enhance business performance. By leveraging AI, businesses can make more informed decisions based on evidence rather than intuition, leading to optimized strategies and increased competitiveness. AI can expedite decision-making, improve accuracy, and foster innovation, making it an invaluable tool for businesses across various industries. As the power and sophistication of AI technology continue to grow, it is clear that its role in driving business success will only become more crucial in the future.

AI'S ABILITY TO PROCESS AND ANALYZE LARGE DATASETS

AI's ability to process and analyze large datasets has revolutionized the way businesses operate and make informed decisions. With the exponential growth of digital information, organizations are constantly faced with a seemingly insurmountable amount of data that needs to be sifted through and analyzed. In the past, this process was time-consuming and required extensive human intervention. AI has emerged as a game-changer in this regard. By harnessing the power of machine learning algorithms and advanced data analytics techniques, AI can efficiently process and make sense of massive amounts of data within a fraction of the time it would take a human.

One of the key advantages of AI in processing large datasets is its speed and efficiency. AI-powered algorithms can rapidly scan through millions, or even billions, of data points in mere seconds. This enables businesses to extract valuable insights and patterns that would otherwise be impossible to detect manually. With AI, organizations can swiftly identify trends, anomalies, and hidden correlations that could potentially make or break their business strategies. This speed and efficiency not only save valuable time but also ensures that businesses can make real-time decisions based on the most up-to-date information.

AI's ability to process large datasets also enhances the accuracy and precision of data analysis. Humans are prone to errors, biases, and limitations when it comes to analyzing vast amounts of data. Our cognitive capabilities are simply not equipped to handle the complexities and intricacies of massive datasets. AI, on the other hand, eliminates these limitations. It can analyze data objectively and consistently, ensuring that the insights derived are unbiased and free from human errors. This increased accuracy in data analysis empowers businesses to make informed decisions based on reliable and precise information, leading to improved business outcomes.

Another significant advantage of AI in processing large datasets is its ability to identify patterns and trends that humans may overlook. Humans are limited by their cognitive biases, as well as their inability to process data at the same scale and speed as AI algorithms. AI algorithms excel at detecting nuanced patterns and trends within massive datasets that may not be immediately apparent to humans. This capability opens up new opportunities for businesses to capitalize on emerging trends, spot market shifts, and gain a competitive edge. By leveraging AI's analytical capabilities, businesses can uncover hidden insights and make data-driven decisions that enhance their overall performance and bottom line. AI's ability to process large datasets also enables businesses to personalize and tailor their offerings to individual customers. In today's data-driven economy, businesses are constantly collecting vast amounts of customer data from various sources, such as social media, online browsing habits, and purchase history. Manually analyzing this data to gain actionable insights for personalized marketing campaigns can be a nearly impossible task. AI algorithms, on the other hand, can seamlessly process and analyze this massive trove of customer data, allowing businesses to understand their customers on a much deeper level. With this understanding, businesses can create highly personalized and targeted marketing strategies that resonate with individual customers, leading to enhanced customer satisfaction and increased sales.

AI's ability to process large datasets also plays a crucial role in enhancing the overall efficiency and productivity of businesses. By automating data analysis processes, AI eliminates the need for manual intervention and streamlines workflows. This frees up valuable human resources, allowing them to focus on complex tasks that require higher-level cognitive abilities. AI can continuously learn and improve its analytical capabilities over time. As it processes more and more data, it can identify patterns, optimize processes, and make data-driven recommendations that further improve business efficiency. In this way, AI becomes a valuable asset for businesses seeking to multiply their results by maximizing productivity and streamlining operations. AI's ability to process and analyze large datasets has transformed the way businesses operate and make informed decisions. With its speed, accuracy, ability to identify patterns, personalize offerings, and enhance overall efficiency, AI has become an indispensable tool for businesses across various industries. By harnessing the power of AI, organizations can unlock valuable insights hidden within massive datasets, empowering them to make data-driven decisions that multiply their business results. As the digital era continues to generate vast amounts of data, the role of AI in processing and analyzing this data will only become more critical in ensuring business success in the future.

BENEFITS OF DATA-DRIVEN DECISION-MAKING IN TERMS OF IMPROVED ACCURACY AND STRATEGIC ADVANTAGE

Data-driven decision-making has increasingly become a crucial aspect of business strategy, as it offers numerous benefits in terms of improved accuracy and strategic advantage. One key advantage of data-driven decision-making is its ability to enhance accuracy. By utilizing data to make informed decisions, businesses can minimize the risk of basing their choices on anecdotal evidence or personal biases. This is particularly important in complex business environments where decisions are often influenced by numerous factors and variables. With data-driven decision-making, businesses can rely on concrete evidence and statistical analysis to make choices that are more likely to yield positive outcomes. This improved accuracy not only enhances the decision-making process itself but also contributes to achieving desired business outcomes.

Data-driven decision-making provides businesses with a strategic advantage. In today's highly competitive business landscape, strategic decision-making plays a crucial role in determining the success or failure of an organization. By utilizing data to inform strategic choices, businesses can gain a deeper understanding of market trends, consumer behavior, and industry dynamics. This allows them to identify opportunities and potential risks, enabling them to adapt their strategies accordingly. For instance, through data analysis, businesses can identify emerging market trends or shifts in customer preferences, allo-wing them to respond proactively and gain a competitive edge. Data-driven decision-making enables businesses to assess the effectiveness of their strategies and make necessary adjust-ments in real-time, ensuring they stay ahead of the competition. Data-driven decision-making promotes efficiency and cost-ef-fectiveness. Traditional decision-making processes often rely on gut instinct and limited information, which can lead to inefficient resource allocation and unnecessary expenses. In contrast, data-driven decision-making enables businesses to optimize re-source allocation and streamline operations. By analyzing data, businesses can identify areas of inefficiency, such as bottlenecks in production processes or underperforming marketing cam-paigns, allowing them to make informed decisions on how to rectify these issues. This efficient use of resources not only re-duces costs but also enhances overall operational effectiveness. For instance, by utilizing data to optimize supply chain mana-gement, businesses can reduce inventory costs, improve delivery times, and enhance customer satisfaction. Data analysis can identify areas for process improvement, enabling businesses to automate repetitive tasks and allocate resources more effi-ciently. Data-driven decision-making fosters a culture of ac-countability and transparency within organizations. By relying on data to make decisions, businesses can establish clear me-trics and goals, ensuring that decisions are aligned with specific objectives. This promotes accountability by holding individuals and teams responsible for achieving these targets. Data-driven decision-making facilitates the transparent sharing of informa-tion and insights within organizations. By making data accessible to relevant stakeholders, businesses can ensure that decisions are based on shared information and understanding. This shared knowledge and transparency contribute to a more collaborative and productive work environment, where decisions are made collectively, and individuals are empowered to contribute their ideas and insights. Data-driven decision-making offers numerous benefits in terms of improved accuracy and strategic advantage. By relying on data, businesses can enhance the accuracy of their decisions, minimizing the risk of bias or anecdotal evidence. This improved accuracy not only enhances the decision-making process itself but also contributes to achieving desired business outcomes. Data-driven decision-making provides businesses with a strategic advantage by enabling them to gain a deeper understanding of market trends, customer behavior, and industry dynamics. By adapting their strategies based on data analysis, businesses can identify opportunities and gain a competitive edge in today's highly competitive business landscape. Data-driven decision-making promotes efficiency and cost-effectiveness by optimizing resource allocation and streamlining operations. Data-driven decision-making fosters a culture of accountability and transparency within organizations, ensuring that decisions are aligned with specific objectives and based on shared knowledge and understanding. Embracing data-driven decision-making is essential for businesses looking to multiply their results and achieve sustainable success in an increasingly data-rich world.

B. UTILIZING AI ALGORITHMS FOR PERSONALIZED RECOMMENDATIONS

One of the most significant applications of AI algorithms in business is their ability to provide personalized recommendations to customers. Personalized recommendations have become essential in today's competitive market, as they not only improve customer satisfaction but also drive sales and customer loyalty. AI algorithms can analyze vast amounts of data, including customer preferences, purchase history, and behavior patterns, to generate personalized recommendations that cater to each individual's specific needs and preferences. By understanding individual customer preferences, businesses can deliver targeted product suggestions and promotions, leading to increased sales and revenue. AI algorithms can leverage sophisticated machine learning techniques to continuously learn and improve recommendations based on customer interactions and feedback. These algorithms can adapt and become more accurate over time, enhancing the overall customer experience. For example, an e-commerce website can use AI algorithms to analyze a customer's browsing behavior, previous purchases, and demographic information to generate personalized product recommendations. By taking into account factors such as the customer's preferred brands, sizes, colors, and styles, the AI algorithm can present a tailored list of product suggestions that are more likely to resonate with the customer's preferences.

AI algorithms can analyze a customer's journey across various touchpoints and channels to create a seamless and personalized experience. For instance, a customer may interact with a business through multiple channels, such as a website, mobile app, or social media. AI algorithms can integrate and analyze data from these different channels to gain a holistic understanding of the customer's preferences and behaviors. This enables businesses to deliver consistent recommendations across all channels, ensuring a consistent and personalized customer experience, regardless of the platform or device being used.

In addition, AI algorithms can play a crucial role in improving cross-selling and upselling opportunities. By understanding customer preferences and purchase history, AI algorithms can identify related products that complement the customer's previous purchases or align with their interests. This not only boosts sales but also enhances the customer's perception of the business. For instance, an AI algorithm can suggest accessories or compatible products to accompany a customer's recent purchase, increasing the average order value and providing a more comprehensive solution to the customer's needs. AI algorithms can analyze and leverage customer feedback and reviews to generate more relevant and accurate recommendations. By considering the sentiments expressed in customer reviews, businesses can identify common preferences and address potential pain points. This enables AI algorithms to refine their recommendations and tailor them based on customer sentiment, leading to more personalized and context-aware suggestions. AI algorithms can identify emerging trends and preferences by analyzing large volumes of reviews, helping businesses stay ahead of the competition and adapt their offerings accordingly. Implementing AI algorithms for personalized recommendations requires a robust and scalable infrastructure to handle the vast amount of data involved. Businesses need to invest in powerful computing resources and storage capabilities to efficiently process and analyze data in real-time. Businesses should prioritize data privacy and security, as collecting and analyzing customer data comes with ethical considerations. Transparent data handling practices and stringent security measures are essential to build trust with customers and comply with data protection regulations.

Utilizing AI algorithms for personalized recommendations offers businesses a powerful tool to enhance the customer experience, drive sales, and foster customer loyalty. By analyzing vast amounts of customer data, AI algorithms can generate tailored recommendations that cater to each individual's preferences. This not only increases customer satisfaction but also improves cross-selling and upselling opportunities. AI algorithms can analyze feedback and reviews to provide more accurate recommendations, while also identifying emerging trends and preferences. Businesses must ensure a robust infrastructure and prioritize data privacy and security to effectively leverage AI algorithms for personalized recommendations. By implementing these technologies, businesses can multiply their results and gain a competitive edge in the market.

HOW AI ALGORITHMS CAN ANALYZE CUSTOMER BEHAVIOR TO PROVIDE PERSONALIZED RECOMMENDATIONS

One significant way to multiply business results with Artificial Intelligence (AI) is by utilizing AI algorithms to analyze customer behavior and provide personalized recommendations. In today's digital age, businesses gather vast amounts of data about their customers, including their preferences, purchase history, and online behavior. Without the proper tools to analyze this data, businesses may struggle to understand their customers' needs and wants effectively. AI technology, particularly AI algorithms, can sift through this wealth of data and extract valuable insights to help businesses streamline their marketing and sales strategies. AI algorithms have the ability to process large datasets quickly and efficiently. They can analyze a customer's behavior across various touchpoints, such as website visits, social media interactions, and online purchases. By examining these data points, AI algorithms can identify patterns, trends, and correlations that may not be apparent to human analysts. For example, an AI algorithm can detect that a customer who frequently buys running shoes also tends to purchase sports accessories like fitness trackers. Armed with this knowledge, businesses can tailor their marketing messages to highlight complementary products or offer personalized promotions based on the customer's interests and preferences. AI algorithms can continuously learn and adapt based on new data inputs. This allows them to provide increasingly accurate recommendations over time. By constantly updating their models, AI algorithms become more attuned to each customer's unique preferences, making their recommendations more valuable and relevant. For instance, well-known online retailers like Amazon and Netflix leverage AI algorithms to provide personalized recommendations to their customers. These algorithms consider a customer's browsing history, past purchases, and even feedback and ratings given by the customer to suggest products or movies that align with the customer's taste. This level of personalization not only enhances the customer experience but also increases the likelihood of conversion and repeat purchases. AI algorithms can analyze customers' behavior in real time, enabling businesses to deliver personalized recommendations at the right moment. This capability is particularly valuable in the e-commerce sector, where timing is crucial. For instance, if an AI algorithm detects that a customer frequently adds items to the shopping cart but ultimately abandons the purchase, it can trigger a real-time recommendation or offer a personalized discount to incentivize the customer to complete the transaction. By leveraging AI algorithms to interpret customer behavior in real-time, businesses can seize opportunities to engage with customers and enhance their experience, ultimately driving sales and fostering customer loyalty.

Another advantage of AI algorithms in analyzing customer behavior is their ability to identify outliers and anomalies. These algorithms can detect unusual customer patterns or behaviors that may indicate a potential issue or a change in customer preferences. For example, if an AI algorithm notices that a long-time customer has drastically reduced their purchasing frequency or switched to a competitor, it can flag this change to the business.

Promptly identifying and addressing such deviations can help businesses prevent customer churn and retain their customer base. Not only do AI algorithms have the power to identify outliers, but they can also identify correlations between customer behavior and external factors, such as changes in consumer trends or macroeconomic conditions. By considering these broader contextual factors, businesses can gain a more comprehensive understanding of customer behavior and make informed decisions to adapt their offerings accordingly.

Leveraging AI algorithms to analyze customer behavior and provide personalized recommendations has the potential to significantly multiply business results. These algorithms can sift through vast datasets to identify patterns and correlations, enabling businesses to tailor their marketing strategies and offer personalized promotions. With the ability to continuously learn and adapt, AI algorithms improve the accuracy and relevance of their recommendations over time. Real-time analysis of customer behavior also allows businesses to deliver recommendations at the right moment, driving engagement and conversions. The detection of outliers and correlations with external factors provides businesses with valuable insights to prevent customer churn and adapt to changing market conditions. Implementing AI algorithms in analyzing customer behavior is a powerful approach to boosting business outcomes in the digital age.

BENEFITS OF PERSONALIZED RECOMMENDATIONS IN TERMS OF CUSTOMER SATISFACTION AND INCREASED SALES

Personalized recommendations have become a significant advantage for businesses in terms of enhancing customer satisfaction and driving increased sales. By leveraging the power of artificial intelligence (AI) algorithms, companies can tailor their recommendations to meet the unique preferences and needs of each individual customer. This personalized approach not only provides customers with better product options but also deepens their engagement with the brand, ultimately leading to a higher level of satisfaction. When customers feel that a company understands their tastes and preferences, they are more likely to trust and continue doing business with that company. Personalized recommendations help increase sales by making the shopping experience more efficient and enjoyable. By presenting customers with products that align with their interests, businesses can significantly reduce search time and eliminate overwhelming choices, leading to faster decision-making. This streamlined process results in higher conversion rates and increased revenue for the business.

C. ENHANCING DECISION-MAKING THROUGH AI-POWERED ANALYTICS

One of the most significant ways in which businesses can multiply their results through artificial intelligence (AI) is by enhancing their decision-making capabilities using AI-powered analytics. Traditionally, decision-making in businesses heavily relied on human expertise and intuition, which often led to suboptimal outcomes due to the limitations of human cognition. With the advancements in AI technology, businesses now have the opportunity to leverage the power of data-driven decisions.

AI-powered analytics refers to the use of AI algorithms to analyze vast amounts of data and generate actionable insights for decision-making. These algorithms are capable of identifying patterns, trends, and correlations within the data, which humans may easily overlook. By applying machine learning techniques, AI algorithms can continuously learn from new data to improve their decision-making capabilities over time.

The use of AI-powered analytics can enhance decision-making in various functional areas of business, such as sales, marketing, operations, and finance. For instance, in sales and marketing, AI algorithms can analyze customer data to identify buying patterns, preferences, and trends. This information can then be used to optimize sales and marketing strategies, target specific customer segments, and personalize customer experiences. By understanding customer needs and predicting their behavior, businesses can make more informed decisions about pricing, product assortment, and promotional activities, thereby maximizing their revenue potential. In operations, AI-powered analytics can help businesses improve their productivity and efficiency. By analyzing operational data, such as supply chain, manufacturing, and logistics data, AI algorithms can identify bottlenecks, optimize workflows, and enhance resource allocation. For example, by analyzing historical production data, AI algorithms can identify production inefficiencies and suggest process improvements, leading to cost savings and improved productivity.

AI-powered analytics can be utilized in financial decision-making, where accuracy and speed are crucial. AI algorithms can analyze financial data, market trends, and macroeconomic indicators to predict stock prices, manage investment portfolios, and assess risk. This can greatly assist businesses in making informed financial decisions, such as investment and portfolio allocation, mergers and acquisitions, and risk management. By leveraging AI-powered analytics, businesses can reduce the likelihood of financial losses and maximize their returns.

AI-powered analytics can enhance strategic decision-making by providing businesses with valuable insights into their competitive landscape. AI algorithms can analyze market data, industry reports, and social media sentiment to assess market trends, evaluate competitor strategies, and identify new opportunities. Armed with this information, businesses can develop robust strategies, enter new markets, and gain a competitive edge.

AI-powered analytics can enable businesses to make proactive, data-driven decisions rather than relying on reactive decision-making. By continuously monitoring data in real-time, AI algorithms can detect anomalies, anticipate changes in customer behavior, and identify potential risks or opportunities. This proactive approach can help businesses stay ahead of their competitors, mitigate risks, and capitalize on emerging trends.

It is essential to acknowledge that AI-powered analytics is not a panacea for decision-making in businesses. While AI algorithms can process vast amounts of data quickly, they are still limited by the quality and relevance of the data fed into them. Businesses must ensure the accuracy and reliability of data sources to derive meaningful insights. Ethical considerations must be taken into account when using AI-powered analytics, such as data privacy, bias, and transparency. To gain trust and acceptance from both employees and customers, businesses must be transparent about their data collection and usage practices and ensure that their AI algorithms operate ethically.

AI-powered analytics has the potential to significantly enhance decision-making in businesses and multiply their results. By leveraging AI algorithms to analyze vast amounts of data, businesses can gain actionable insights, improve productivity, optimize strategies, and make more informed financial decisions. It is essential for businesses to ensure the accuracy and relevance of data sources and consider ethical considerations to effectively harness the power of AI-powered analytics. When used responsibly, AI-powered analytics can be a valuable tool for businesses to gain a competitive edge and achieve desired outcomes.

USE OF AI ANALYTICS TOOLS TO UNCOVER PATTERNS AND CORRELATIONS IN DATA

With the increasing amount of data being generated in today's digital age, businesses are recognizing the importance of utilizing AI analytics tools to uncover patterns and correlations within this vast pool of information. AI analytics tools employ sophisticated algorithms and machine learning techniques to analyze data sets, identify trends, and make predictions. By utilizing these tools, organizations are able to gain invaluable insights into their customers, operations, and overall market trends. For instance, an e-commerce company can use AI analytics tools to identify customer preferences and purchasing behaviors, enabling them to personalize marketing campaigns and offer targeted recommendations. This not only enhances customer satisfaction but also improves sales and revenue. AI analytics tools can also help businesses identify operational inefficiencies and streamline processes. By analyzing various data points, such as production rates and resource allocation, organizations can identify bottlenecks in their operations and take proactive measures to address them. This leads to improved productivity, cost savings, and a competitive edge in the market. AI analytics tools can uncover correlations between different variables that may not be immediately apparent to humans. For example, by analyzing customer data, a retail company may discover that customers who purchase certain products are also more likely to buy other related items. Armed with this knowledge, businesses can develop targeted upselling and cross-selling strategies. The use of AI analytics tools allows businesses to harness the power of data and make data-driven decisions, resulting in increased efficiency, improved customer satisfaction, and ultimately, multiplied business results.

BENEFITS OF AI-POWERED ANALYTICS IN FACILITATING DATA-DRIVEN DECISION-MAKING

One of the most significant benefits of incorporating AI-powered analytics in business operations is its ability to facilitate data-driven decision-making. In today's fast-paced and highly competitive business environment, making informed decisions based on accurate and relevant data has become crucial for the success and growth of enterprises. AI-powered analytics tools can process large volumes of data, extract meaningful insights, and present them in a format that is easily understandable and actionable for decision-makers. These analytics tools are capable of identifying patterns, trends, and correlations within data sets that may go unnoticed by human analysts due to the sheer volume and complexity of the information. This enables businesses to gain valuable insights into consumer behavior, market trends, and operational efficiency, allowing them to make informed decisions that maximize business outcomes. For example, AI-powered analytics tools can analyze customer data to identify their preferences, buying patterns, and potential lifetime value. This data can then be used to segment customers into different groups and develop personalized marketing strategies to target each segment more effectively. By tailoring marketing efforts to specific customer needs and preferences, businesses can increase customer satisfaction, enhance brand loyalty, and ultimately generate higher revenues. AI-powered analytics can also be used to optimize supply chain management by analyzing production, sales, and inventory data in real-time. This allows businesses to predict demand, manage inventories more efficiently, and reduce costs associated with overstocking or stockouts. By making data-driven decisions based on these insights, businesses can streamline their operations, improve customer service, and achieve higher profitability. AI-powered analytics can contribute to enhancing business intelligence by providing real-time data monitoring and reporting capabilities. Traditional methods of data analysis are often time-consuming and prone to errors, as they rely on manual processing and interpretation of data. AI algorithms can process data in real-time, generating accurate reports and alerts to key stakeholders. This enables businesses to monitor the performance of various departments, track key performance indicators, and identify potential issues or opportunities promptly. For example, AI-powered analytics tools can monitor website traffic, customer engagement, and conversion rates to provide insights into the effectiveness of marketing campaigns. By continuously monitoring these metrics, businesses can make data-driven decisions to optimize marketing strategies and improve their return on investment. AI-powered analytics can contribute to risk management by identifying potential threats and vulnerabilities in business operations. By analyzing data from various sources such as financial transactions, customer behaviors, and social media sentiment, AI algorithms can detect patterns indicating fraudulent activities or cybersecurity breaches. This early identification of risks allows businesses to take proactive measures and mitigate potential damages. For instance, a bank can use AI-powered analytics to identify suspicious transactions and flag them for further investigation, preventing financial losses and maintaining customer trust. The integration of AI-powered analytics into business operations offers a range of benefits, particularly in facilitating data-driven decision-making. By processing and analyzing large volumes of data, AI-powered analytics can extract meaningful insights that enable businesses to make informed decisions based on accurate and relevant information. This supports businesses in gaining valuable insights into customer behavior, market trends, and operational efficiency, leading to increased revenues and profitability. AI-powered analytics can contribute to monitoring business performance in real-time, enhancing business intelligence and risk management capabilities. It is evident that AI-powered analytics has the potential to transform the way businesses operate and achieve long-term success in today's data-driven world. In today's rapidly evolving business landscape, companies are constantly seeking innovative ways to gain a competitive edge and maximize their performance. One particularly effective strategy that has gained prominence in recent years is harnessing the power of artificial intelligence (AI) to multiply business results. AI, as a disruptive technology, has the potential to revolutionize various aspects of business operations and drive significant improvements in productivity, efficiency, and profitability. One way AI can help businesses multiply their results is through enhanced customer experience and personalization. By leveraging AI-powered algorithms, companies can collect and analyze vast amounts of customer data to gain valuable insights into their preferences, behaviors, and needs. This information can then be utilized to tailor product recommendations, marketing communications, and customer interactions in a highly personalized manner. By delivering a more personalized and engaging experience, businesses can improve customer satisfaction and loyalty, leading to increased sales and repeat business. AI can greatly enhance operational efficiency and streamline business processes, resulting in significant cost savings and productivity gains. For instance, AI-powered automation can be leveraged to perform repetitive and time-consuming tasks, such as data entry, customer support, and inventory management. This not only frees up valuable time and resources but also minimizes the risk of human error. AI can also be used to optimize supply chain management, by analyzing real-time data, predicting demand patterns, and optimizing inventory levels. This enables businesses to reduce costs, minimize waste, and improve overall operational efficiency.

AI can empower businesses to make data-driven decisions that are both accurate and timely. Through machine learning algorithms and predictive analytics, AI can analyze vast quantities of data to identify patterns, trends, and insights that may not be immediately apparent to human analysts. This allows businesses to make informed decisions based on real-time data, rather than relying on intuition or past experience alone. By leveraging AI, companies can ensure that they are making decisions based on the most relevant and accurate information available, leading to improved strategic planning and more successful outcomes. AI can be used to optimize marketing and advertising efforts, resulting in higher conversion rates and revenue growth. AI-powered algorithms can analyze customer data to identify target audiences, segment them based on various criteria, and develop highly targeted marketing campaigns. AI can also enhance ad targeting and optimization, by leveraging real-time data and feedback to adjust ad placements, content, and messaging in real-time. By delivering the right message to the right audience at the right time, businesses can significantly improve conversion rates, maximize return on ad spend, and ultimately increase revenue. Another significant way AI can multiply business results is through improved risk management and fraud detection. By analyzing large volumes of data and applying advanced algorithms, AI can identify potential risks or fraudulent activities in real-time, allowing businesses to take proactive measures to mitigate them. For example, AI can be used to detect unusual patterns and anomalies in financial transactions, flagging potentially fraudulent activities for further investigation. By leveraging AI in risk management, businesses can enhance their ability to identify and address potential risks and threats, ultimately safeguarding their reputation and financial well-being. AI can also play a pivotal role in enhancing innovation and driving new business opportunities. By analyzing data from multiple sources, AI can identify market trends, customer demands, and emerging patterns that may not be immediately apparent to human analysts. This can enable businesses to uncover untapped market opportunities, develop new product offerings, and identify potential areas for growth and expansion. AI can also be employed to assist with research and development efforts, by automating time-consuming tasks such as data analysis, simulations, and experimentation. By leveraging AI in innovation processes, businesses can accelerate their pace of innovation, drive new revenue streams, and gain a competitive edge. AI has the potential to multiply business results in various ways. By enhancing customer experience and personalization, improving operational efficiency, enabling data-driven decision-making, optimizing marketing efforts, enhancing risk management, and driving innovation, AI can revolutionize business operations and drive significant improvements in performance. As companies continue to discover the transformative power of AI, its adoption and integration will become increasingly vital for businesses seeking to gain a competitive edge in today's dynamic marketplace.

IV. ENHANCING CUSTOMER EXPERIENCES

Enhancing customer experiences is a crucial aspect of business success, and AI technology offers significant opportunities to achieve this goal. In today's highly competitive market, businesses are constantly striving to provide exceptional customer service that not only meets but exceeds consumer expectations. AI has the potential to revolutionize customer experiences by enabling businesses to gain deep insights into customer preferences and behaviors. By integrating AI capabilities into their operations, companies can personalize their offerings, tailor their marketing strategies, and optimize their overall customer journey. One way AI can enhance customer experiences is through personalization. AI algorithms can analyze vast amounts of customer data, including their purchase history, browsing patterns, and social media activities. By harnessing this information, businesses can gain a comprehensive understanding of individual customer preferences and interests. With this knowledge, companies can deliver customized content, products, and recommendations that resonate with each customer on a personal level. This personalized approach not only increases customer satisfaction but also drives customer loyalty and repeat business. AI can optimize marketing strategies by enabling businesses to target the right customers with the right message at the right time. AI-powered tools can analyze consumer data and identify patterns and trends that can inform marketing decisions. For example, AI algorithms can predict when and what customers are most likely to purchase, allowing businesses to time their promotions and incentives appropriately. This targeted approach maximizes the effectiveness of marketing campaigns, leading to higher conversion rates and revenue growth.

AI-powered chatbots and virtual assistants can greatly improve customer support and service. Gone are the days when customers had to wait for extended periods to speak with a representative or navigate through complex phone menus. AI chatbots, equipped with natural language processing capabilities, can provide quick and accurate answers to customer inquiries, thereby reducing response times and enhancing customer satisfaction. These chatbots can also handle routine tasks, such as order tracking or refund processing, freeing up human representatives to focus on more complex customer issues. AI-powered virtual assistants, such as Amazon's Alexa or Apple's Siri, can interact with customers in a conversational manner, offering recommendations, answering questions, and providing personalized assistance. This seamless integration of AI technology into customer support not only enhances the overall customer experience but also reduces operational costs for businesses.

Another way AI can enhance customer experiences is by improving the overall customer journey. AI algorithms can analyze vast quantities of customer data to identify pain points, bottlenecks, or areas for improvement in the customer experience. By uncovering hidden patterns or anomalies, businesses can implement targeted strategies to address these issues and streamline the customer journey. For example, AI algorithms can analyze customer feedback to identify common complaints or frustrations, enabling companies to improve their products, services, or processes accordingly. By continuously collecting and analyzing customer data, businesses can stay attuned to customer needs and preferences, allowing them to enhance their offerings and adapt to changing market trends.

AI can enhance customer experiences by enabling businesses to offer augmented reality (AR) or virtual reality (VR) experiences. AR and VR technologies have the potential to transport customers to immersive and interactive environments, providing unique and engaging experiences. For instance, automotive companies can use AR to allow customers to virtually test drive vehicles, while furniture retailers can use AR to enable customers to visualize how specific items would look in their homes. By leveraging AI-powered AR and VR technologies, businesses can provide memorable and enjoyable experiences that differentiate them from their competitors and leave a lasting impression on customers. Enhancing customer experiences is a critical aspect of business success, and AI technology offers tremendous opportunities to achieve this goal. By leveraging AI's capabilities, businesses can personalize their offerings, optimize their marketing strategies, streamline the customer journey, and provide augmented or virtual reality experiences. As the competition intensifies, integrating AI systems into business processes can give companies a competitive edge by delivering superior customer experiences that drive customer loyalty, repeat business, and ultimately, business growth.

A. PERSONALIZING CUSTOMER INTERACTIONS THROUGH AI

Another way to multiply business results with AI is by personalizing customer interactions. Personalization has become a crucial aspect of successful customer engagement, as it allows companies to tailor their offerings to individual customers' specific needs and preferences. AI-powered technology has greatly enhanced the ability to personalize customer interactions, providing businesses with valuable insights and enabling the delivery of highly tailored experiences. Through AI, companies can collect and analyze vast amounts of customer data, including purchasing history, browsing behavior, and social media activity, to gain a nuanced understanding of each customer. This data can then be used to create personalized recommendations, offers, and marketing campaigns. For instance, AI-powered chatbots can interact with customers in real-time, using natural language processing algorithms to understand and respond to their queries and concerns. These chatbots can provide personalized recommendations based on the customer's previous purchases and preferences, enhancing the overall customer experience. AI-powered analytics can segment customers into different groups based on their traits, allowing businesses to develop targeted marketing strategies. By personalizing customer interactions, businesses can foster stronger customer relationships, increase customer loyalty, and ultimately drive sales and revenue.

It is important to strike the right balance between personalization and privacy concerns to ensure customer trust.

AI'S ABILITY TO COLLECT AND ANALYZE CUSTOMER DATA FOR PERSONALIZED COMMUNICATION

AI's ability to collect and analyze customer data for personalized communication is another key aspect of its transformative potential in multiplying business results. In today's highly competitive market, businesses must strive to create meaningful and personalized experiences for their customers in order to foster loyalty and drive revenue growth. AI offers a unique solution to this challenge by enabling businesses to gather and analyze vast amounts of customer data, thereby gaining valuable insights into individual preferences, behaviors, and purchasing patterns. Through sophisticated machine learning algorithms, AI can process and interpret this data to identify trends, patterns, and correlations that may have been otherwise overlooked. By understanding their customers on a deeper level, businesses can tailor their communication strategies and marketing campaigns to better resonate with their target audience, leading to increased engagement, conversion rates, and ultimately, revenue. AI can facilitate real-time personalized communication by dynamically adapting its messages based on customer interactions and preferences. Through the use of chatbots and virtual assistants, businesses can provide instant and relevant responses to customer queries or concerns, creating a seamless and efficient customer experience. This personalized approach not only enhances customer satisfaction but also fosters a sense of trust and loyalty, as customers feel understood and valued by the business. AI can help businesses identify potential upsell or cross-sell opportunities by analyzing customer data and predicting future purchasing behaviors. By leveraging this information, businesses can offer targeted recommendations or promotions to their customers, increasing the chances of generating additional sales and revenue. AI's ability to collect and analyze customer data for personalized communication has the potential to revolutionize the way businesses interact with their customers, leading to improved customer satisfaction, loyalty, and ultimately, business growth.

BENEFITS OF PERSONALIZED CUSTOMER INTERACTIONS IN TERMS OF INCREASED CUSTOMER LOYALTY AND SATISFACTION

Personalized customer interactions have significant benefits in terms of increased customer loyalty and satisfaction. In today's competitive business landscape, ensuring customer retention and building long-term relationships is vital for sustained success. Through AI-powered personalization, businesses can deliver tailored experiences to their customers, making them feel valued, understood, and appreciated. Firstly, personalized interactions foster a sense of loyalty among customers. When a business takes the time to understand individual customer preferences, needs, and desires, it demonstrates a commitment to delivering a personalized experience. This level of attention not only increases customer satisfaction but also instills a sense of trust and loyalty towards the brand. According to a study conducted by Deloitte, 36% of consumers expressed a willingness to pay more for personalized products or services, indicating the strong influence of personalized interactions on customer loyalty. Secondly, personalized interactions contribute to enhanced customer satisfaction. By leveraging AI technologies, businesses can collect and analyze vast amounts of customer data, including previous purchases, browsing history, and preferences. With this information, companies can tailor their communication, recommendations, and offerings to meet each customer's unique needs and interests. This level of personalization minimizes the risk of irrelevant or uninteresting content, ultimately leading to higher levels of customer satisfaction. AI-powered personalization enables businesses to anticipate customer needs and proactively address them. For instance, an e-commerce platform can use AI algorithms to suggest personalized product recommendations based on a customer's browsing history, leading to a more satisfying shopping experience. Such proactive engagement shows customers that the company cares about their needs, which can significantly increase satisfaction levels and build long-term customer loyalty. Personalized interactions foster a deeper emotional connection between customers and businesses. By treating customers as individuals rather than just another transaction, businesses can create a more personal and meaningful relationship. This emotional bond plays a pivotal role in customer loyalty and can significantly impact their decision-making process. When customers feel emotionally connected to a brand, they are more likely to choose it over competitors, even if the prices or offerings are similar. According to a survey by Forrester, emotional connections influenced 79% of customer decisions and had a stronger influence than factors like price and convenience. Personalized interactions not only create emotional connections but also enable businesses to personalize their marketing efforts, positioning their brand as one that truly understands and cares about its customers. For example, a personalized email or a targeted ad that reflects a customer's interests and preferences can evoke positive emotions and strengthen the bond between the customer and the brand. In addition to increasing customer loyalty and satisfaction, personalized interactions also have a direct impact on business revenue and growth. According to a study by Epsilon, 80% of customers are more likely to make a purchase when businesses offer personalized experiences. This correlation between personalization and purchase behavior highlights the potential revenue opportunities that businesses can unlock with AI-powered personalization strategies. Personalized customer interactions can lead to higher average order values and customer lifetime values. When customers receive personalized recommendations or offers, they are more likely to add additional items to their cart or make repeat purchases, increasing both the value of their individual transactions and their long-term value as customers. Personalized interactions generate positive word-of-mouth and referrals. Satisfied customers who have had personalized experiences are more likely to recommend the brand to friends, family, and colleagues, significantly expanding the business's customer base. They become brand advocates who willingly promote the brand through testimonials or social media, contributing to organic growth without the need for extensive marketing efforts.

Personalized customer interactions through AI-powered personalization strategies have numerous benefits for businesses. They foster customer loyalty by making customers feel valued and understood, ultimately leading to increased customer retention. Personalized interactions also contribute to enhanced customer satisfaction by delivering tailored experiences that address individuals' unique needs and interests. Personalized interactions create emotional connections, further strengthening the bond between customers and businesses. Beyond the intangible benefits, personalization has a direct impact on business revenue and growth. Through personalized experiences, businesses can increase purchase behavior, average order values, and customer lifetime values. Satisfied customers who have experienced personalization are more likely to become brand advocates, generating positive word-of-mouth and referrals. As technology continues to advance, the role of AI in personalization will become increasingly crucial in enabling businesses to multiply their results and achieve sustainable success.

B. IMPROVING CUSTOMER SERVICE WITH AI-POWERED CHATBOTS

In addition to streamlining customer service processes, AI-powered chatbots have the potential to greatly improve the overall customer experience. These chatbots are capable of delivering personalized and timely assistance to customers, thus effectively addressing their queries and concerns. With the help of natural language processing algorithms, these chatbots can understand and interpret customer inputs, enabling them to provide accurate and relevant responses. This level of responsiveness not only reduces customer waiting times but also enhances their satisfaction levels. AI-powered chatbots can operate 24/7, ensuring round-the-clock availability to cater to the needs of global customers residing in different time zones. This accessibility eliminates the frustration of customers facing support limitations and enables businesses to maintain a competitive edge in the market. Chatbots can be integrated with existing customer relationship management (CRM) systems, enabling them to access customer history and previous interactions. This integration allows chatbots to provide a more personalized experience by offering tailored recommendations, product suggestions, and targeted promotions based on customers' previous purchases and preferences. By leveraging AI algorithms, chatbots can not only provide generic responses but also analyze customer sentiments and emotions, helping businesses identify potential issues or concerns even before customers explicitly state them. This proactive approach allows businesses to deliver proactive solutions promptly, thereby increasing customer loyalty and promoting positive word-of-mouth. AI-powered chatbots prove to be invaluable tools in improving customer service and enhancing the overall customer experience.

AI CHATBOTS CAN PROVIDE INSTANT AND ACCURATE RESPONSES TO CUSTOMER QUERIES

AI chatbots have revolutionized the way businesses interact with customers by providing instant and accurate responses to customer queries. These chatbots are powered by advanced algorithms and artificial intelligence technology, enabling them to understand and respond to customer inquiries in real-time. With the ability to process vast amounts of data and learn from customer interactions, AI chatbots can deliver quick and precise answers to a wide range of questions. This not only enhances customer satisfaction but also improves operational efficiency and productivity for businesses. One of the key benefits of AI chatbots is their ability to provide instant responses to customer queries. Unlike human agents, chatbots are available 24/7 and can handle multiple customer inquiries simultaneously. This means that customers no longer have to wait for extended periods to get their questions answered, resulting in a significant improvement in response time. AI chatbots can process information at lightning speed, allowing them to quickly analyze the query and provide a relevant and accurate response. This instantaneous feedback creates a seamless customer experience, leading to higher customer engagement and retention rates.

AI chatbots are designed to provide accurate responses consistently. These chatbots are trained on vast amounts of data and are capable of understanding natural language, context, and user intent. By leveraging machine learning algorithms, they can continuously improve their performance and accuracy over time.

This enables them to accurately interpret customer queries, even when faced with ambiguous or complex questions. Unlike human agents who may make errors or misunderstand customer inquiries, AI chatbots consistently deliver precise and reliable responses. This level of accuracy not only enhances customer satisfaction but also reinforces the trust and credibility of the business. Another advantage of using AI chatbots is their proficiency in handling a wide range of customer queries. AI chatbots can be programmed to understand and respond to various types of inquiries, including product information, order status, troubleshooting, and frequently asked questions. They can access and retrieve information from the business's knowledge base or integrate with other systems to gather relevant data. This versatility means that customers can find answers to their questions without having to navigate through complex websites or wait for human assistance. AI chatbots can take on the role of virtual assistants, guiding customers through the buying process or resolving their issues efficiently. AI chatbots can integrate with other business systems, such as customer relationship management (CRM) software, e-commerce platforms, or inventory management systems. This integration enables them to access and retrieve real-time information, such as customer order history, preferences, or product availability. By leveraging this data, AI chatbots can provide personalized recommendations or tailor their responses to each customer's unique needs. This level of personalization enhances the customer experience by making interactions more relevant and meaningful. It also contributes to increased customer loyalty and repeat business.

AI chatbots can contribute to improved operational efficiency and productivity for businesses. By automating customer inquiries and routine tasks, businesses can free up valuable human resources to focus on more complex or strategic activities. AI chatbots can handle a significant volume of customer inquiries concurrently, reducing the workload on human agents and minimizing the need for additional staff. They can provide instant responses without the need for breaks or vacations, ensuring round-the-clock customer support. This not only allows businesses to deliver superior customer service but also reduces operational costs and overheads. AI chatbots have emerged as powerful tools to provide instant and accurate responses to customer queries. Their ability to process large amounts of data, learn from interactions, and deliver quick and precise answers has transformed customer service in a variety of industries. By offering instantaneous feedback, ensuring accuracy, and handling a wide range of inquiries, AI chatbots significantly enhance customer satisfaction and engagement. They contribute to improved operational efficiency, productivity, and cost savings for businesses. As AI chatbot technology continues to advance, businesses should seize this opportunity to multiply their results and deliver exceptional customer experiences.

BENEFITS OF CHATBOTS IN TERMS OF IMPROVED CUSTOMER SERVICE AND REDUCED RESPONSE TIMES

An essential aspect of any successful business is providing exceptional customer service. In the digital era, advancements in artificial intelligence (AI) have brought about significant changes in the way businesses interact with their customers. One application of AI that has revolutionized customer service is the use of chatbots. Chatbots are computer programs designed to simulate human conversation and provide instant responses to customer queries. In recent years, chatbots have gained popularity due to their ability to deliver improved customer service and reduce response times. One of the primary benefits of chatbots is their 24/7 availability, ensuring uninterrupted support for customers. Unlike human agents who have limited working hours, chatbots can engage with customers at any time, day or night. This round-the-clock availability ensures that customers receive prompt assistance, regardless of the time zone they are in. The promptness of chatbot responses significantly reduces wait times, enhancing customer satisfaction. In the fast-paced digital world, individuals expect instant answers to their queries, and chatbots deliver just that. By swiftly addressing customer concerns, chatbots enable businesses to provide efficient customer service, leading to increased customer loyalty and retention. Another advantage of chatbots is their ability to handle multiple customer conversations simultaneously, thereby boosting productivity. Unlike human agents who can only handle a limited number of conversations at once, chatbots excel at multitasking. This feature allows businesses to serve a larger customer base without compromising the quality of customer service. Chatbots can quickly retrieve information from vast databases to provide accurate and precise responses to customer queries. This eliminates the need for customers to wait or be transferred to different departments, saving valuable time for both parties involved. By leveraging chatbots' multitasking capabilities, businesses can effectively manage their customer support operations, increasing efficiency and reducing costs. Alongside their efficiency, chatbots contribute to improved customer service through their consistent delivery of information and adherence to company guidelines. Unlike human agents who may inadvertently deviate from company policies or provide inconsistent answers, chatbots can be programmed to strictly adhere to predefined guidelines. This ensures a standardized customer service experience across all interactions, regardless of the human agent's knowledge or expertise. Chatbots follow a predetermined set of rules to provide accurate and reliable responses, reducing the likelihood of misinformation or confusion for customers. Consequently, businesses can be confident in the quality of service their customers receive, enhancing their reputation and brand image. Chatbots can be personalized to suit individual customers' needs and preferences. By analyzing customer data and previous interactions, chatbots can provide personalized recommendations and suggestions, leaving customers feeling valued and understood. This personalized touch establishes a positive emotional connection between the customer and the business, fostering customer loyalty and repeat business. Chatbots can adapt their responses based on customer feedback, continuously improving and enhancing the customer experience. Chatbots offer businesses valuable insights into customer preferences, needs, and pain points. As chatbots engage in conversations with customers, they can collect and analyze data on customer behavior, preferences, and frequently asked questions. This information can be used to identify patterns and trends, helping businesses understand their target audience better. Armed with these insights, businesses can develop targeted marketing campaigns, create tailored products and services, and improve their overall customer service strategy. Chatbots have proven to be a valuable asset for businesses seeking to enhance customer service and reduce response times. Their 24/7 availability ensures uninterrupted support and prompt assistance for customers, increasing customer satisfaction and loyalty. Chatbots' multitasking capabilities and access to large databases allow businesses to efficiently manage customer support operations, improving productivity and reducing costs. The consistent delivery of information and adherence to company guidelines ensure a standardized and reliable customer service experience. By personalizing responses and analyzing customer data, chatbots establish an emotional connection with customers and provide businesses with valuable insights. As businesses continue to leverage AI technologies like chatbots, the benefits of improved customer service and reduced response times will undoubtedly pave the way for enhanced business results.

C. CUSTOMIZING PRODUCTS AND SERVICES WITH AI

Customizing products and services with AI holds tremendous potential for businesses wanting to enhance customer satisfaction and drive revenue growth. Through the use of advanced algorithms and machine learning, AI can analyze vast amounts of customer data to gain valuable insights into individual preferences and behaviors. This data can then be leveraged to offer personalized recommendations, tailor-made products, and seamless experiences that meet the unique needs of each customer. For instance, AI-powered chatbots can gather information about a customer's preferences and past purchases, enabling businesses to suggest relevant products and services in real-time. AI can analyze customer feedback and sentiment analysis to identify areas of improvement and implement changes that lead to enhanced customer experiences. By harnessing the power of AI, businesses can go beyond the one-size-fits-all approach and provide customers with highly customized solutions that not only meet but exceed their expectations. The ability to personalize products and services helps businesses create a deeper emotional connection with customers and fosters loyalty and advocacy. When customers feel that a company understands and caters to their unique needs, they are more likely to remain loyal and become brand advocates, ultimately resulting in increased sales and customer retention. Customized products and services can command premium pricing, leading to improved profit margins for businesses.

One industry that has greatly benefited from the customization capabilities of AI is the fashion and beauty sector. AI-powered virtual try-on features allow customers to visualize how different clothing items or makeup products would look on them without physically trying them on. By analyzing a customer's features and style preferences, AI can generate personalized recommendations that match their taste and body type, ensuring a more satisfying and convenient shopping experience. AI algorithms can also assist in creating custom-made clothing, helping businesses cater to diverse body shapes and sizes, ultimately reducing returns and enhancing customer satisfaction. AI can aid in trend forecasting by analyzing social media data and fashion trends, enabling businesses to introduce new products and styles that resonate with their target audience.

Apart from the fashion industry, other sectors such as e-commerce, hospitality, and healthcare are also leveraging AI to customize their offerings. E-commerce giants like Amazon and Netflix use AI-driven recommendation engines to offer their customers personalized product suggestions and curated content, increasing customer engagement and driving sales. In the hospitality industry, AI-powered virtual concierges can enhance the hotel experience by providing guests with tailored recommendations for dining, sightseeing, and entertainment based on their preferences and previous interactions. This personalized approach helps hotels differentiate themselves from competitors and create memorable experiences that build customer loyalty. AI can optimize healthcare services by enabling personalized treatment plans and medication recommendations based on patients' medical history and genetic data. By customizing healthcare services, AI can help improve patient outcomes and enhance the overall efficiency of healthcare delivery.

While the customization potential of AI is undoubtedly promising, businesses must ensure that they maintain a balance between personalization and privacy. As AI relies heavily on customer data, it is crucial for businesses to prioritize data security and adhere to privacy regulations. Clear communication and transparency regarding data collection and usage can help establish trust with customers, ensuring that their information is handled responsibly and ethically. Businesses must ensure that they obtain explicit consent from customers before utilizing their data for personalization purposes. By respecting customers' privacy concerns while offering personalized experiences, businesses can build strong, long-lasting relationships with their customers. Customizing products and services with AI has the potential to revolutionize the way businesses operate and interact with their customers. By leveraging AI algorithms and machine learning, businesses can offer personalized recommendations, tailor-made products, and seamless experiences that cater to the individual needs and preferences of customers. This customization capability helps businesses foster customer loyalty, increase sales, and improve profit margins. Businesses must also prioritize data security and privacy to maintain customer trust. Through responsible and ethical implementation, the customization potential of AI can pave the way for enhanced customer satisfaction and drive business growth in various industries.

UTILIZING AI ALGORITHMS TO TAILOR PRODUCTS AND SERVICES TO INDIVIDUAL CUSTOMER PREFERENCES

One way to multiply business results with AI is by utilizing AI algorithms to tailor products and services to individual customer preferences. AI has the power to analyze large amounts of data and extract meaningful insights, which can then be used to personalize the customer experience. By understanding each customer's preferences, businesses can offer targeted recommendations, create personalized marketing campaigns, and develop products that cater to specific needs and desires.

The first step in utilizing AI algorithms to tailor products and services is gathering customer data. This includes demographics, purchasing history, browsing behavior, and even social media activity. The more data a business has on its customers, the better it can understand their preferences and provide personalized recommendations. This data can be collected through various channels, such as online surveys, purchase histories, and social media monitoring tools.

Once the data is collected, AI algorithms can be used to analyze and interpret the information. Machine learning algorithms can identify patterns and correlations within the data, allowing businesses to understand customer preferences and predict future behavior. For example, if a customer frequently purchases sports apparel, the algorithm can identify this preference and recommend similar products or inform the business to create targeted marketing campaigns promoting sports apparel.

The next step is utilizing these insights to tailor products and services to individual customer preferences. Personalization can take various forms, depending on the type of business and the products or services offered. For e-commerce companies, personalization can involve recommending products based on past purchases or browsing history. These recommendations can be displayed on the website or sent via personalized email newsletters. Retailers can also leverage AI algorithms to create targeted promotions and discounts for specific customers, increasing their chances of making a purchase.

In addition to product recommendations, AI can also help businesses personalize their marketing campaigns. By understanding individual customer preferences, businesses can create customized messages and promotions that resonate with each customer. For example, if a customer has shown an interest in eco-friendly products, a business could create a marketing campaign highlighting their sustainable practices or offering discounts on environmentally friendly products. This level of personalization not only increases the likelihood of conversion but also strengthens customer loyalty and engagement.

AI can be used to develop products that cater to specific customer needs and desires. By analyzing customer data and preferences, businesses can identify gaps in the market and create innovative solutions that meet those needs. For example, if a significant number of customers prefer organic skincare products, an AI algorithm can highlight this demand, prompting the business to develop a new line of organic skincare products. This approach ensures that businesses are always offering products and services that are relevant and desirable to their target audience. Personalization through AI algorithms also extends to customer service. Chatbots powered by AI can offer personalized assistance to customers by answering questions, providing product recommendations, and resolving issues. These chatbots can utilize customer data to understand the specific context and needs of each customer, resulting in a more efficient and tailored customer service experience. This not only improves customer satisfaction but also reduces the workload on customer service teams, allowing them to focus on more complex tasks.

Leveraging AI algorithms to tailor products and services to individual customer preferences offers numerous benefits for businesses. By collecting and analyzing customer data, businesses can gain valuable insights into customer preferences and behavior. These insights can then be used to personalize product recommendations, marketing campaigns, and even create new products. This level of personalization not only increases conversion rates but also enhances customer satisfaction and loyalty. AI-powered customer service can offer personalized assistance, improving the overall customer experience. Utilizing AI algorithms to tailor products and services allows businesses to meet the evolving needs and desires of their customers, thereby multiplying their business results.

BENEFITS OF CUSTOMIZATION IN TERMS OF INCREASED CUSTOMER ENGAGEMENT AND SALES

Another significant advantage of utilizing AI-powered customization is the potential for increased customer engagement and ultimately leading to higher sales. Customization enables businesses to deliver personalized experiences to individual customers, catering to their specific needs and preferences. By leveraging data analytics and AI algorithms, companies can gain valuable insights into customer behavior, preferences, and purchasing patterns. Armed with this information, businesses can create tailored marketing campaigns that resonate with customers on a much deeper level. Personalized messages, promotions, and recommendations can be delivered to customers at the right time and through the most appropriate channels, increasing the likelihood of engagement and purchase.

When customers feel that a brand understands their preferences and is actively working to meet their unique requirements, it creates a sense of loyalty and trust. By offering products or services that are tailored to the individual customer, businesses can foster a stronger emotional connection with their target audience. This emotional connection translates to increased customer engagement, as customers are more likely to actively interact with the brand and provide valuable feedback. Through these interactions, businesses can gain further insights into customer preferences, allowing them to refine their offerings and provide an even more personalized experience.

In the context of e-commerce, AI-powered customization can significantly enhance the online shopping experience. By analyzing customer data and behavior, businesses can create dynamic websites that adapt to each individual user. AI algorithms can present customers with personalized product recommendations based on their browsing history, purchase behavior, and even their preferences from similar customers. This level of personalization makes the online shopping experience more convenient and enjoyable for customers, leading to increased engagement and sales. By leveraging AI-powered chatbots, businesses can provide instant and personalized customer support, answering inquiries and providing assistance in real-time. This improves customer satisfaction and increases the likelihood of repeat purchases. In traditional retail settings, AI-powered customization can also play a crucial role in augmenting customer engagement. By utilizing facial recognition technology, businesses can identify individual customers as they enter their stores. With this information, AI algorithms can create personalized shopping experiences, such as tailored product suggestions, personalized discounts, or even targeted in-store advertising. This level of individualized attention makes customers feel valued and encourages them to spend more time and money in the store. Businesses can utilize AI-powered inventory management systems to ensure that the products customers desire are always in stock, further enhancing the customer experience and increasing sales.

By enabling customers to customize their products, businesses can create a unique selling proposition that sets them apart from competitors. AI-powered customization platforms can allow customers to personalize various aspects of a product, such as its design, color, or size. This level of customization empowers customers to create a product that uniquely reflects their preferences and personality. Not only does this enhance customer satisfaction, but it also provides a valuable marketing tool. Customers are more likely to share and promote products that they have personally customized, leading to increased brand awareness and word-of-mouth referrals. This organic, customer-driven marketing can significantly contribute to increased sales and business growth. AI-powered customization offers various benefits in terms of increased customer engagement and sales. Through the utilization of data analytics and AI algorithms, businesses can deliver personalized experiences and tailor their marketing campaigns to individual customers. This level of personalization fosters a stronger emotional connection with customers, leading to increased engagement and loyalty. In the realm of e-commerce, AI-powered customization enhances the online shopping experience by providing personalized product recommendations and instant customer support. In traditional retail settings, AI-powered customization augments customer engagement through personalized shopping experiences and inventory management. By enabling customers to customize products, businesses can create a unique selling proposition that sets them apart from competitors while also benefiting from organic customer-driven marketing. AI-powered customization has the potential to revolutionize business operations and drive significant growth by delivering personalized experiences to customers. One of the most remarkable ways to multiply business results with AI is through the incorporation of machine learning models. Machine learning is a subset of AI that focuses on the ability of computer systems to learn and improve automatically from experience without being explicitly programmed. By leveraging machine learning models, businesses can gain valuable insights and predictions based on large amounts of data. For instance, companies can use predictive analytics models to forecast market trends, optimize pricing strategies, and identify potential risks. These models can analyze historical data patterns, customer behavior, economic indicators, and other relevant factors to generate accurate predictions about future outcomes. This not only enables businesses to make more informed decisions but also helps them identify untapped opportunities and implement proactive strategies. Machine learning models can be trained to recognize patterns and anomalies in data, leading to greater efficiency in fraud detection, cybersecurity, and risk management. By automating these tasks, businesses can save substantial time and resources while enhancing the accuracy and effectiveness of their processes. Another area where machine learning has proven to be extremely beneficial is in personalizing customer experiences. AI-powered recommendation systems can analyze vast amounts of customer data, such as past purchases, browsing history, and preferences, to provide personalized recommendations, offers, and advertisements. This helps businesses increase customer engagement, loyalty, and overall satisfaction. Machine learning can be used to automate customer support services through chatbots and virtual assistants. These automated systems can accurately understand and respond to customer queries, provide relevant information, and resolve issues in a timely manner. By doing so, businesses can improve customer service while reducing costs associated with manual support staff. In the realm of marketing, AI can revolutionize advertising campaigns by targeting the right audience with personalized messages. Through advanced algorithms and machine learning techniques, businesses can optimize their advertising efforts by identifying and focusing on the most valuable customer segments. AI can analyze large and diverse datasets, such as demographics, interests, online behavior, and purchase history, to build accurate customer profiles. By leveraging these insights, businesses can run highly targeted and effective advertising campaigns that yield higher conversion rates and return on investment. In addition, AI can help businesses streamline and automate their supply chain management processes. For instance, by using machine learning models, businesses can accurately forecast demand, optimize inventory levels, and improve logistics operations. This not only reduces costs associated with excess inventory and stockouts but also enhances customer satisfaction through timely and accurate deliveries. AI can assist businesses in improving their decision-making process. By analyzing vast amounts of data from various sources, AI can provide executives and managers with real-time insights and recommendations. This supports data-driven decision-making, allowing businesses to adapt quickly to changing market conditions, make informed strategic choices, and stay ahead of the competition. For example, AI-powered data analytics platforms can provide businesses with valuable insights about customer behavior, market trends, and competitor strategies. By analyzing these insights, businesses can identify areas for improvement, develop effective marketing campaigns, and make informed pricing and product development decisions. AI can also play a crucial role in enhancing the effectiveness and efficiency of internal processes. By automating routine and repetitive tasks, businesses can free up employees' time to focus

on more strategic and creative activities. For instance, AI-powered software can automate data entry, document processing,
and financial analysis, reducing errors and increasing productivity. AI can improve employee training and development. Intelligent tutoring systems can personalize learning experiences
based on each individual's strengths, weaknesses, and learning
style. This leads to better skill acquisition, knowledge retention,
and overall performance. AI has the potential to greatly multiply
business results across various areas and functions. By leveraging machine learning models, businesses can gain valuable insights and predictions, personalize customer experiences, optimize advertising campaigns, automate processes, improve decision-making, and enhance employee development. The incorporation of AI technologies can help businesses gain a competitive edge, increase efficiency, reduce costs, and ultimately
achieve their goals with greater success.

V. OVERCOMING CHALLENGES OF AI IMPLEMENTATION

Implementing AI within a business environment is not without its challenges. Firstly, one of the major roadblocks to successful AI implementation is the lack of understanding and skepticism among employees. Many individuals fear that AI will replace their jobs or diminish their importance within the organization. This resistance can be overcome through effective communication and training initiatives. By clarifying the role of AI as a tool to augment human intelligence rather than replace it, employees can be encouraged to embrace the technology and recognize its benefits. Another significant hurdle is the availability and quality of data. AI algorithms rely heavily on large and diverse datasets to function effectively. Many organizations struggle with data fragmentation and siloed information, making it difficult to gather sufficient data for AI implementation. This challenge can be addressed through data integration initiatives aimed at consolidating and organizing data from different sources. Organizations must ensure the quality and accuracy of their data, as inaccurate or incomplete data can result in biased algorithms and misleading insights. Ethical considerations pose a challenge to the successful implementation of AI. The use of AI raises concerns regarding privacy, security, and algorithmic bias. Organizations must navigate complex ethical dilemmas to ensure that AI technologies are used responsibly and in line with legal and societal norms. This can be achieved by establishing clear guidelines and policies around data privacy and security, as well as implementing safeguards to prevent bias and discrimination in AI models. Technical challenges also impede the implementation of AI. Developing and maintaining AI systems requires advanced technological expertise and infrastructure. Many organizations lack the necessary technical capabilities and resources, making it challenging to implement and maintain AI solutions. To overcome this hurdle, partnerships with AI technology providers or hiring AI experts can provide organizations with the necessary knowledge and support. Collaboration with external experts can accelerate the implementation process and ensure the long-term success of AI initiatives.

Cultural resistance within organizations can be a significant barrier to AI implementation. Some employees may be resistant to change or lack the necessary digital literacy to fully embrace AI technologies. Overcoming this challenge requires a cultural shift within the organization. Organizations should foster a culture of continuous learning and innovation, providing employees with the necessary training and resources to understand and utilize AI technologies effectively. Creating a supportive and inclusive environment will encourage employees to embrace AI and drive its successful implementation. Cost considerations pose a challenge to the widespread adoption of AI. Implementing AI technologies can require significant financial investment, especially for small and medium-sized enterprises. The high costs associated with AI implementation, including infrastructure, training, and maintenance, can deter organizations from embarking on an AI journey. To overcome this challenge, businesses can explore cost-sharing models, such as cloud-based AI solutions or subscription-based services, which provide access to AI technologies without a significant upfront investment. Organizations can prioritize AI initiatives based on their potential return on investment, gradually scaling up as they witness tangible results. The successful implementation of AI within a business environment requires addressing several challenges. Overcoming employee skepticism, data availability and quality, ethical considerations, technical expertise, cultural resistance, and cost considerations are all crucial for the widespread adoption and utilization of AI technologies. By actively addressing these challenges and fostering a supportive and inclusive environment, organizations can harness the transformative power of AI to drive innovation, enhance decision-making processes, and multiply their business results.

A. DATA MANAGEMENT AND PRIVACY CONCERNS

As companies increasingly rely on AI algorithms to analyze large volumes of data, it is essential to address the challenges associated with data management and privacy concerns. Firstly, data management becomes crucial as businesses gather vast amounts of data from various sources. This includes customer information, purchase history, social media interactions, and browsing patterns. Consequently, organizations must establish robust data management systems that ensure data security, accuracy, and accessibility. Implementing efficient data governance frameworks that outline data usage, storage, and retention policies can enhance data management practices. Companies should focus on adopting robust data integration strategies to ensure that diverse data sources can be effectively incorporated into AI systems. Apart from data management, privacy concerns are also significant as organizations handle personal and sensitive information. The collection and utilization of personal data, particularly in AI applications like recommender systems or targeted advertising, have raised concerns about privacy violation and data misuse. To address these concerns, businesses must ensure compliance with data protection regulations, such as the General Data Protection Regulation (GDPR) in Europe or the California Consumer Privacy Act (CCPA) in the United States. These regulations mandate companies to obtain explicit user consent for data collection and processing, as well as provide individuals with the right to access, modify, or delete their personal information. Dedicating resources to privacy protection measures, such as encryption, anonymization, and access controls, is crucial to maintain public trust and minimize the risks of data breaches or unauthorized access. Data management and privacy concerns are closely linked as effective data management practices can help address privacy issues. By incorporating privacy by design principles into AI systems, companies can embed data protection measures from the earliest stages of development. This includes implementing techniques like differential privacy, which adds noise to data to prevent re-identification of individuals. By applying these privacy-enhancing technologies, organizations can strike a balance between utilizing valuable data for AI algorithms and safeguarding individuals' privacy. Adopting privacy-preserving data sharing frameworks, such as federated learning, allows multiple organizations to collaborate and train AI models collectively without sharing raw data. This way, privacy concerns can be mitigated while benefiting from shared knowledge and insights. While data management and privacy concerns pose challenges, they also present opportunities for businesses to differentiate themselves. Companies that can demonstrate effective data management practices and robust privacy protection measures gain a competitive advantage in today's data-driven economy. Public awareness about data privacy has increased substantially in recent years, leading customers to prioritize companies that respect their privacy rights. Hence, businesses that prioritize data protection and actively communicate their privacy measures can build trust, loyalty, and a positive brand image. Emphasizing customer-centric data management approaches, such as providing transparency about data usage and empowering individuals with control over their data, can further strengthen customer relationships and enhance reputation. Organizations that invest in data management and prioritize privacy can tap into the growing market for ethical AI solutions. With the rise in AI applications across industries, there is a demand for transparent, fair, and accountable AI systems. By ensuring responsible data management practices and complying with privacy regulations, businesses can offer ethical AI solutions that prioritize user privacy and mitigate biases or discrimination. These ethical AI solutions that prioritize data management and privacy can attract socially conscious customers, foster innovation, and drive sustainable growth.

Data management and privacy concerns are critical aspects of maximizing the benefits of AI technologies for businesses. The effective management of vast amounts of data and addressing privacy concerns not only ensures compliance with regulations but also helps build customer trust and loyalty. By adopting strong data governance frameworks, integrating diverse data sources, and incorporating privacy by design principles, companies can strike a balance between utilizing data for AI algorithms and safeguarding individuals' privacy. Prioritizing data management and privacy can differentiate businesses, attract customers, and tap into the growing market for ethical AI solutions. Organizations must recognize and address data management and privacy concerns to multiply their business results with AI.

ISSUES RELATED TO DATA COLLECTION, STORAGE, AND PRIVACY

As businesses increasingly rely on artificial intelligence (AI) to multiply their results, the collection and storage of vast amounts of data have become essential for effective implementation. This practice raises several ethical and legal questions that demand careful consideration. One key issue pertains to the methods by which data is acquired. While some information may be willingly provided by individuals, such as when signing up for a service or making a purchase, obtaining data without explicit consent is a violation of privacy. Businesses must ensure that they are adhering to relevant laws and regulations regarding data collection, such as the European Union's General Data Protection Regulation (GDPR), which emphasizes the importance of obtaining informed consent. Businesses must address concerns surrounding the storage of collected data. With the advent of cloud computing, the ability to store vast amounts of data has become both cost-effective and convenient. This centralized approach also poses risks, as it becomes crucial to safeguard the stored data from unauthorized access or potential breaches. This necessitates stringent security measures to protect sensitive information, including the use of encryption and firewalls. Businesses should regularly update their security protocols to stay ahead of emerging threats and ensure the safe storage of data. Privacy concerns also arise from the potential misuse of collected data. In an AI-driven business environment, data is often used to train machine learning models or make personalized recommendations to users. While this can enhance user experiences and business outcomes, there is a fine line between leveraging data and infringing on privacy rights. Businesses must establish clear guidelines regarding the use of personal data, ensuring that it is anonymized and aggregated whenever possible. By doing so, they can mitigate the risk of inadvertently revealing sensitive information while still reaping the benefits of data-driven AI applications. Transparency is another critical aspect related to data collection, storage, and privacy. Businesses should strive to maintain open and honest communication with their users, informing them about the types of data being collected and how it will be utilized. By being transparent, businesses can establish trust with their users and build long-lasting relationships. Transparency can help prevent any potential backlash or legal repercussions stemming from a lack of explicit consent or undisclosed data practices. To address privacy concerns, the concept of data minimization has gained traction. Data minimization entails collecting only the necessary information required for specific purposes, thus reducing the amount of potentially sensitive data being stored. By practicing data minimization, businesses can minimize their exposure to privacy risks and limit the potential impact of a data breach. This principle aligns with the notion of privacy by design, which advocates for privacy considerations to be incorporated into the system architecture from the outset, rather than being an afterthought. Businesses must be aware of emerging concerns surrounding data protection. As technology evolves, so do the associated challenges. For instance, the rise of Internet of Things (IoT) devices poses new risks in terms of data collection and privacy. The interconnected nature of these devices can lead to the accumulation of extensive personal information, requiring businesses to implement appropriate safeguards and device-level security measures. Advancements in AI bring the ethical dilemma of deepfakes and their potential impact on privacy. Deepfakes, which involve manipulating videos or images to create realistic yet fake content, underscore the urgency for businesses to develop strategies to combat disinformation and protect individuals' privacy.

The issues related to data collection, storage, and privacy are paramount in today's AI-driven business landscape. To effectively multiply their results with AI, businesses must prioritize the ethical and legal implications of data collection, ensuring that consent is obtained when acquiring information and following established regulations. Storage of data must be approached with caution and robust security measures to safeguard sensitive information from unauthorized access. Privacy concerns can be addressed by anonymizing and aggregating personal data whenever possible, while maintaining transparency with users about data practices. The principles of data minimization and privacy by design are essential to minimize risks and protect individuals' privacy. Businesses must remain vigilant in adapting to emerging concerns, such as those posed by IoT devices or the ethical implications of deepfakes. Only by addressing these issues can businesses harness the full potential of AI while ensuring the protection of privacy rights.

STRATEGIES FOR ENSURING ETHICAL AND SECURE USE OF CUSTOMER DATA

Strategies for ensuring ethical and secure use of customer data are crucial in today's data-driven business landscape. Firstly, businesses must focus on establishing clear ethical guidelines and policies that govern the collection, storage, and use of customer data. These guidelines should prioritize transparency and informed consent, ensuring that customers are fully aware of how their data will be used and have the option to opt-out if they wish. Businesses should invest in robust data security measures, such as encryption and firewalls, to protect customer data from unauthorized access and breaches. Regular audits and security assessments can help identify vulnerabilities and ensure compliance with data protection regulations. Secondly, businesses should consider adopting privacy-enhancing technologies (PETs) to safeguard customer data. Technologies such as differential privacy and homomorphic encryption enable businesses to analyze customer data while preserving privacy. By anonymizing and aggregating data, businesses can gather valuable insights without compromising individuals' identities. Thirdly, businesses must prioritize data governance practices that promote responsible data use. This includes implementing stringent data access controls and conducting regular data audits to ensure compliance with internal policies and external regulations. Companies should also establish robust data sharing agreements when collaborating with third parties, ensuring that these partners have adequate measures in place to protect customer data. Fourthly, businesses should cultivate a culture of data ethics and privacy awareness within their organizations. This includes providing comprehensive training programs to educate employees on the importance of ethical data practices and privacy protection. Employees should be equipped with the necessary knowledge and tools to handle customer data responsibly. Businesses should appoint internal data protection officers who can oversee compliance efforts, address customer concerns, and act as a point of contact for data privacy issues. Businesses should proactively engage with customers and seek their feedback to improve data privacy practices. This can involve soliciting consent and preferences at regular intervals, providing clear and concise privacy notices, and offering customers greater control over their data through user-friendly privacy settings. By actively involving customers in the conversation surrounding data privacy, businesses can build trust, enhance customer relationships, and differentiate themselves in the marketplace. Ethical and secure use of customer data is essential for businesses today. By establishing ethical guidelines, investing in data security measures, adopting PETs, implementing data governance practices, cultivating a culture of data ethics, and engaging with customers, businesses can ensure the responsible and secure use of customer data. These strategies not only protect customer privacy but also enhance customer trust, foster long-term relationships, and drive business growth.

B. SKILLS AND TALENT GAPS IN AI ADOPTION

One significant challenge facing organizations in their journey towards adopting AI is the scarcity of skilled professionals who possess the necessary expertise to effectively implement and manage AI systems. While the field of AI has experienced rapid advancements and innovations in recent years, the supply of professionals with the requisite skills and knowledge has struggled to keep up. As a result, businesses often find themselves grappling with a talent gap, hindering their progress in AI adoption. AI is a complex and constantly evolving field, demanding a diverse skill set that includes expertise in machine learning, data science, programming languages, and algorithm development. The scarcity of individuals who possess proficiency in these areas is one of the main reasons for the skills gap in AI adoption. Many organizations struggle to find professionals who can comprehend and navigate the complexities of AI algorithms, as well as effectively apply statistical models to analyze vast amounts of data. Keeping pace with new developments in AI requires professionals who are continuously learning and updating their skills, resulting in a constant need for ongoing training and development programs within organizations.

In addition to the technical skills required, organizations also face a shortage of talent who possess the necessary business acumen to bridge the gap between AI technologies and their practical implementation in a business context. While technical expertise is vital, it must be complemented by a deep understanding of the organization's specific goals, strategy, and processes. This fusion of technical and strategic knowledge enables AI professionals to identify and leverage AI opportunities that align with the business's objectives, therefore maximizing the potential for AI adoption to deliver tangible results. Unfortunately, individuals who possess this holistic skill set are in high demand, leading to a shortage of talent in this regard.

The scarcity of skilled professionals in AI poses a significant challenge for businesses looking to adopt AI technologies. Their ability to successfully implement and derive value from AI is directly tied to the availability of professionals who possess the requisite skills. Consequently, organizations must invest in attracting and retaining top talent in AI by offering competitive salaries, providing ongoing learning and development opportunities, and creating a supportive work environment that fosters innovation and collaboration. Companies can partner with academic institutions and industry organizations to establish internships, apprenticeships, and mentorship programs to nurture a pipeline of skilled professionals who can contribute to AI adoption efforts. Another approach to addressing the skills and talent gaps in AI adoption is through upskilling existing employees. This approach not only helps businesses overcome the shortage of skilled professionals but also enables them to leverage the knowledge and experience of their existing workforce. Organizations can establish AI training programs to equip employees with the necessary technical skills and knowledge to effectively engage with AI technologies. Upskilling programs can range from short-term workshops to more extensive certification courses, designed to cater to employees at different levels of technical proficiency. By investing in their existing workforce, organizations can harness the collective potential of their employees, fostering a culture of continuous learning and innovation.

Organizations can look to leverage external resources such as consultants and freelancers to bridge the skills and talent gaps temporarily. This approach allows businesses to tap into a diverse pool of specialized professionals who can provide expertise in specific AI domains or projects. By engaging external resources, organizations can access immediate skills and experience while also providing an opportunity for internal employees to learn and collaborate with these experts, thus enhancing their own skill set and contributing to the long-term talent development strategy of the organization. The skills and talent gaps in AI adoption are significant hurdles that organizations must overcome to effectively harness the potential of AI technologies. The scarcity of skilled professionals who possess the necessary technical knowledge and business acumen poses a challenge for businesses seeking to adopt and implement AI systems. Organizations can address these gaps by investing in attracting and retaining top talent, upskilling their existing workforce, and leveraging external resources. By investing in the development of a skilled workforce, businesses can enhance their AI adoption efforts, multiplying their potential to achieve meaningful business results through AI.

CHALLENGES IN RECRUITING AND TRAINING EMPLOYEES WITH AI EXPERTISE

One significant challenge faced by organizations in the realm of AI is the recruitment and training of employees with expertise in this field. With the ever-increasing demand for AI talent, competition among companies to attract individuals with the necessary skills has become intense. The scarcity of qualified professionals capable of working with AI technologies poses a hurdle to the efficient implementation of AI strategies within businesses. The rapid evolution of AI techniques and algorithms requires continuous learning and upskilling for existing employees. This implies that organizations need to invest in comprehensive training programs to ensure their workforce remains up to date with the latest advancements in AI. Developing such training initiatives is not a straightforward task. It requires careful consideration of individual needs and learning styles, as well as significant financial and time investments. Providing employees with the opportunity to gain practical experience with AI technologies can be challenging due to the cost and availability of specific tools and resources. Thus, organizations must address these recruitment and training challenges to harness the benefits of AI effectively. In the area of recruitment, organizations often face difficulties in attracting AI professionals due to their high demand and limited supply. The increasing reliance on AI technologies across various industries has created a fierce competition for the limited talent pool available. As a result, organizations must adopt innovative recruitment strategies to appeal to highly

skilled candidates. This includes offering competitive salary packages, flexible work arrangements, and attractive professional
development opportunities. Organizations can establish partnerships with academic institutions and research centers to promote AI education and encourage students to pursue careers in
this field. Collaborating with these institutions can help organizations identify and recruit talented individuals who possess the
desired AI expertise. Organizations can explore global talent
markets, leveraging remote work options and visas to access AI
skilled professionals from diverse locations. Such recruitment
strategies can significantly enhance the ability of organizations
to acquire the necessary AI talent.

Once employees with AI expertise are recruited, organizations
face the challenge of providing them with the necessary training
to keep their skills up to date. The field of AI is constantly evolving, with breakthroughs and innovations occurring at a rapid
pace. This necessitates ongoing education and training to ensure
employees remain well-versed in the latest AI techniques and
algorithms. Organizations can address this challenge by developing comprehensive training programs that focus on both theoretical knowledge and practical applications of AI. These programs should cover various aspects of AI, including machine
learning, natural language processing, computer vision, and
deep learning. Organizations can encourage their employees to
participate in external training programs, workshops, and conferences to expose them to diverse perspectives and keep them
abreast of emerging trends in the field. By investing in continuous learning initiatives, organizations can foster a culture of
innovation and ensure that their employees are equipped with
the necessary skills to leverage AI effectively.

Another challenge in training employees with AI expertise lies in providing them with practical experience in working with AI tools and technologies. Practical exposure is crucial for employees to develop a deep understanding of AI concepts and gain proficiency in implementing AI solutions. Access to the required tools and resources for hands-on experience can be costly and limited. To overcome this challenge, organizations can establish collaborations with AI technology vendors and research institutions to gain access to cutting-edge AI tools and resources. Organizations can set up dedicated AI labs or innovation centers within their premises to provide employees with a conducive environment for experimentation and learning. These spaces can be equipped with the necessary hardware and software to enable employees to work on AI projects and gain practical experience. By investing in the infrastructure and resources required for practical AI training, organizations can ensure that their employees have the necessary skills and confidence to apply AI techniques in real-world business scenarios.

The recruitment and training of employees with AI expertise pose significant challenges to organizations. The scarcity of AI talent, the need for continuous learning, and the practical exposure required make it crucial for businesses to address these challenges effectively. Organizations must adopt innovative recruitment strategies, such as offering competitive packages and establishing partnerships with academic institutions, to attract highly skilled AI professionals. Developing comprehensive training programs and providing access to practical resources and tools are essential to ensure that employees remain up to date with the latest advancements in AI. By overcoming these challenges, organizations can tap into the immense potential of AI and multiply their business results.

STRATEGIES FOR ADDRESSING SKILLS GAPS AND FOSTERING A CULTURE OF AI ADOPTION

Strategies for addressing skills gaps and fostering a culture of AI adoption require a multifaceted approach that combines training programs, mentorship opportunities, and collaboration among academia, industry, and government entities. Firstly, organizations should invest in comprehensive training programs to bridge the skills gap and equip employees with the necessary knowledge and expertise in AI technologies. These programs should encompass both technical skills, such as programming and data analysis, as well as domain-specific knowledge to ensure employees understand the specific applications of AI within their respective fields. Organizations should offer mentorship programs to pair employees with experienced AI practitioners who can guide them through the learning process and provide valuable insights and real-world application scenarios.

Collaboration among academia, industry, and government entities is essential to create a robust ecosystem that supports AI adoption. Universities can play a vital role in developing curriculum and research programs that focus on AI and related technologies, allowing students to gain hands-on experience and deepen their understanding of AI principles. Industry partnerships with universities can also foster collaborative research projects and internships, providing students with practical exposure to the application of AI in real-world contexts. Government organizations can contribute to fostering a culture of AI adoption by providing funding and support for research initiatives, developing policies that promote AI integration across various sectors, and facilitating partnerships between academia and industry. In order to create a culture of AI adoption, organizations should prioritize creating an environment that encourages experimentation, risk-taking, and continuous learning. This can be achieved through initiatives such as hackathons, innovation challenges, and cross-functional teams that allow employees to explore AI technologies and develop innovative solutions to business challenges. Organizations should also provide dedicated resources, such as access to data and computing infrastructure, to support experimentation and enable employees to gain practical experience with AI tools and techniques.

Fostering a culture of AI adoption requires effective change management strategies and clear communication to ensure employees understand the benefits of AI and are motivated to embrace it. Organizations should proactively communicate the rationale behind AI adoption, emphasizing the potential to enhance productivity, streamline processes, and create new business opportunities. Clear communication channels should be established to address employees' concerns and provide support throughout the adoption process. Organizations should recognize and reward employees who actively engage in AI initiatives, creating incentives for continuous learning and driving a positive culture shift. To maximize the effectiveness of strategies for addressing skills gaps and fostering a culture of AI adoption, organizations should continuously monitor and evaluate their efforts. This can be done through regular assessments of employees' skills and competencies, measuring the impact of training programs, and collecting feedback from employees regarding their experiences and challenges in adopting AI. By gathering data and insights, organizations can identify areas for improvement, refine their strategies, and iterate on their approach to further enhance the adoption of AI.

Addressing skills gaps and fostering a culture of AI adoption requires a comprehensive approach that integrates training programs, mentorship opportunities, collaboration among academia, industry, and government entities, and supportive organizational environments. By investing in the upskilling of employees, developing partnerships with educational institutions, fostering a culture of experimentation and learning, and implementing effective change management strategies, organizations can successfully bridge skills gaps, promote the adoption of AI, and unlock its transformative potential for business growth and innovation.

C. ENSURING TRANSPARENCY AND ACCOUNTABILITY IN AI SYSTEMS

As AI technologies become more pervasive in various sectors, it is imperative to establish mechanisms that promote transparency and accountability in the decision-making processes of these systems. One approach to achieve this is through explainability, where AI systems are designed to provide comprehensible explanations for their outputs. Explainability not only aids in understanding the reasoning behind AI decisions but also facilitates the identification of biases or potential errors. Consequently, designers and users can be held accountable for the system's decisions, ensuring that AI is used responsibly and ethically. Establishing a robust regulatory framework is essential to guarantee transparency and accountability in AI systems. Authorities need to develop guidelines and standards that address the ethical concerns related to AI, such as privacy, fairness, and discriminatory biases. These regulations would require organizations to disclose the algorithms and data used in AI systems, enabling independent audits and assessments. This way, potential biases or ethical issues can be identified and mitigated. Regulatory frameworks should also mandate transparency in the training and development processes of AI systems, ensuring that they are subjected to rigorous testing and validation before deployment. The implementation of accountability mechanisms, such as an AI audit, is essential to ensure adherence to ethical standards. An AI audit would involve evaluating the decision-making processes and outputs of an AI system, assessing its compliance with legal and ethical mandates. This audit can be conducted by independent organizations or regulatory bodies established specifically for AI oversight. By holding organizations accountable for the actions of their AI systems, audits contribute to mitigating risks, promoting transparency, and fostering trust in AI technology. In addition to internal accountability mechanisms, external oversight is crucial to ensuring transparency and accountability in AI systems. Appointing an independent regulatory body responsible for overseeing AI applications can help prevent misuse and ensure compliance with ethical guidelines. This regulatory body can evaluate the design, development, and deployment of AI systems, assess their societal impact, and impose penalties for non-compliance. Through external oversight, organizations are encouraged to prioritize responsible AI practices and remain transparent in their operations. Another critical aspect of ensuring transparency and accountability in AI systems is promoting diversity and inclusion in their development and deployment. By involving diverse perspectives in the design process, potential biases can be identified and mitigated effectively. Diversity in the workforce responsible for developing AI systems can help challenge implicit biases, leading to fairer and more ethical outcomes. Ensuring that the data used to train AI models is representative of diverse populations is also crucial for avoiding discriminatory biases. This can be achieved by proactively collecting diverse and inclusive datasets. Promoting diversity and inclusion not only leads to better AI performance but also helps safeguard against unethical and biased outcomes. Fostering a culture of transparency and accountability within organizations is paramount in ensuring responsible AI practices. Organizations should prioritize creating an environment that encourages individuals to speak up when they notice potential biases or ethical concerns in AI systems. This can be achieved by implementing whistleblower protection policies and anonymous reporting mechanisms. Encouraging open dialogue and facilitating discussions on the ethical implications of AI systems can also promote awareness and accountability among employees. By fostering a culture that values transparency and accountability, organizations can proactively address potential issues and ultimately guarantee the responsible use of AI technology. Ensuring transparency and accountability in AI systems is crucial to address ethical concerns and establish trust in its deployment across various sectors. Achieving transparency can be done through explainability, regulatory frameworks, and external audits. Accountability can be ensured through external oversight, diversity and inclusion in system development, and fostering a culture of transparency within organizations. By implementing these measures, we can create a responsible and ethically grounded AI ecosystem that maximizes business results while safeguarding against potential risks and harms.

THE IMPORTANCE OF EXPLAINING AI DECISIONS AND AVOIDING BIAS

One key aspect that cannot be overlooked when implementing AI technology in business is the importance of explaining AI decisions and avoiding bias. As AI systems become more sophisticated and pervasive, businesses must ensure that these systems can provide transparent explanations for the decisions they make. This is crucial for several reasons. First and foremost, transparency helps build trust between businesses, consumers, and regulators. When a business can clearly explain how and why an AI system arrived at a particular decision, it eliminates uncertainty and skepticism surrounding its use of AI technology. This is especially important in sectors such as healthcare, finance, and law, where the impact of AI decisions can have significant consequences on people's lives.

Explaining AI decisions is not only essential for building trust, but also for addressing potential bias in these systems. AI algorithms are developed based on historical data, which can inadvertently reflect and perpetuate existing biases within society. For instance, if a hiring AI system is trained on historical datasets that favor men over women, it may perpetuate gender bias in the hiring process. By explaining these decisions, businesses can identify and rectify biases in AI systems. It allows businesses to critically analyze the algorithmic bias, correct for it, and ensure fairness and equal opportunities for all individuals.

Explaining AI decisions is necessary for complying with regulatory requirements and ethical standards. As AI technology continues to advance, regulators are increasingly recognizing the importance of transparency in decision-making processes. For instance, the European Union's General Data Protection Regulation (GDPR) explicitly states that individuals have the right to understand the logic behind automated decisions that significantly affect them. This not only emphasizes the importance of explaining AI decisions but also highlights the legal obligations businesses have when deploying AI systems. By proactively explaining AI decisions, businesses can demonstrate their commitment to compliance and ethical practices, thereby avoiding potential legal and reputational risks. Explaining AI decisions opens up opportunities for learning and improvement. When AI systems operate as "black boxes" – providing outputs without any explanation – it becomes challenging to understand how they arrived at those decisions. In contrast, transparent AI systems enable businesses to gather insights and learn from their algorithms. By analyzing the explanations provided by the AI system, businesses can identify areas of improvement and refine their decision-making processes. This iterative approach enables businesses to enhance the accuracy, consistency, and efficiency of their AI systems, leading to better business outcomes. Explaining AI decisions is essential to ensure accountability and mitigate potential harm. As AI technology becomes increasingly integrated into critical decision-making processes, it is crucial to hold businesses accountable for the actions and consequences of their AI systems. If an AI system, for example, determines creditworthiness and denies an individual a loan, the individual has the right to understand the rationale behind this decision. Explaining the AI decision not only allows businesses to justify their actions, but also provides affected individuals with an opportunity to challenge unjust or discriminatory decisions. This promotes fairness, reduces the risk of harm, and protects individuals' rights in the face of increasing automation.

Explaining AI decisions and avoiding bias are of utmost importance when leveraging AI technology in business. Transparency fosters trust between businesses, consumers, and regulators, while also allowing for the identification and rectification of biases in AI systems. Complying with regulatory requirements, demonstrating ethical practices, and avoiding legal risks are additional benefits of explaining AI decisions. Transparent AI systems offer learning opportunities, enabling businesses to continuously improve their decision-making processes. Explaining AI decisions ensures accountability and safeguards individuals' rights by providing them with insights into and opportunities to challenge automated decisions. Businesses should prioritize the development and implementation of systems that can provide transparent explanations for AI decisions, paving the way for responsible and successful AI integration in various industries.

ETHICAL CONSIDERATIONS AND REGULATORY FRAMEWORKS FOR AI IMPLEMENTATION

Ethical considerations and regulatory frameworks play a crucial role in the successful implementation of AI in businesses. As AI continues to advance and become more integrated into various industries, it is imperative to address the ethical implications that arise from its use. One major concern is the potential bias in AI algorithms and decision-making processes. AI systems learn from large amounts of data, and if this data contains biased or unrepresentative information, it can perpetuate and amplify these biases. For instance, if a hiring algorithm is trained on historical data that reflects gender or racial bias, it may inadvertently discriminate against certain groups in the hiring process. It is essential to ensure that AI systems are trained on diverse and unbiased data sets to minimize such biases. Issues such as privacy and data protection need to be considered when implementing AI. As AI systems rely heavily on data collection and analysis, there is a risk of infringing upon individuals' privacy rights. Regulatory frameworks, such as the General Data Protection Regulation (GDPR) in the European Union, aim to protect individuals' rights and establish guidelines for businesses handling personal data. Compliance with such regulations is crucial to ensure that AI implementations adhere to ethical standards and protect users' privacy. Transparency and explainability are vital in AI systems to foster trust and accountability. Many AI algorithms, such as deep learning neural networks, are often considered black boxes, meaning that their decision-making process is not easily understandable by humans. This lack of transparency can be problematic, especially in critical areas such as healthcare or finance. For instance, if an AI system recommends a specific treatment plan for a patient, it is important for healthcare professionals and patients to understand the rationale behind that recommendation. Various approaches, such as interpretable machine learning techniques, are being developed to address this issue and make AI systems more interpretable. Regulations and standards can help ensure that businesses provide adequate explanations for AI-based decisions, allowing individuals to understand the reasoning behind those decisions and identify any potential biases or errors.

The potential impact of AI on employment raises ethical questions that must be addressed. While AI can streamline processes and increase efficiency, it also has the potential to replace human jobs. This raises concerns about the displacement of workers and the potential social and economic implications. It is crucial for businesses to consider the ethical dimensions of AI implementation and take steps to mitigate any negative effects on employees. This may involve reskilling and retraining programs to enable employees to adapt to changing job requirements or implementing measures to ensure a fair distribution of AI-generated benefits among workers. In terms of regulatory frameworks, governments and international organizations are recognizing the need for oversight and governance of AI. The European Commission, for example, has put forward proposals for a legal framework on AI, aiming to ensure that AI is developed and used in a way that complies with fundamental rights and values. These proposals include AI-specific regulation, requirements for high-risk AI systems, and potential fines for non-compliance. Other countries, such as the United States and Canada, are also exploring regulatory approaches to address the ethical and social implications of AI. Collaborative efforts between governments, industry stakeholders, and academia are crucial to establishing ethical and regulatory frameworks for AI implementation. Ethical guidelines and best practices can be developed through multi-stakeholder engagement to ensure that AI is used in a responsible and accountable manner. This involves considering the perspectives of various stakeholders, including industry experts, ethicists, policymakers, and civil society organizations. By working together, these stakeholders can contribute their expertise to shape ethical standards and regulatory frameworks that truly address the social, ethical, and legal challenges surrounding AI implementation. Ethical considerations and regulatory frameworks are fundamental to the responsible implementation of AI in businesses. Addressing concerns around biases, privacy, transparency, employment, and governance is essential to ensure that AI systems are fair, trustworthy, and accountable. Businesses must actively engage with ethical discussions, comply with regulations, and adopt best practices to maximize the positive impact of AI while mitigating any potential risks or negative consequences. Only through a collaborative and proactive approach can we fully harness the potential of AI while upholding ethical principles and safeguarding societal well-being.

In addition to its myriad applications in the business world, artificial intelligence (AI) has proven to be an invaluable tool in multiplying business results. One way in which AI can enhance business outcomes is through its ability to collect and analyze vast amounts of data at an unprecedented speed. With traditional methods, gathering and processing such large quantities of information would be a time-consuming and labor-intensive task. AI-powered algorithms can effortlessly handle enormous volumes of data, providing businesses with valuable insights and enabling them to make informed decisions more efficiently. AI can identify patterns and trends within data sets that might otherwise go unnoticed. By recognizing these patterns, businesses can gain a deeper understanding of customer preferences, market trends, and operational inefficiencies. Armed with this knowledge, companies can make more accurate predictions and develop strategies to optimize their operations and increase profitability. Another way in which AI can multiply business results is through its ability to automate repetitive and mundane tasks. Many businesses have processes that involve repetitive manual work, such as data entry, customer support, and inventory management. These tasks can be time-consuming and prone to human error, leading to inefficiencies and reduced productivity. By employing AI-driven automation tools, businesses can streamline these processes, freeing up valuable time and resources. For instance, chatbots powered by AI can effectively handle customer inquiries, provide instant responses, and even make product recommendations based on specific customer preferences. By automating this aspect of customer support, businesses can ensure consistent and efficient service, leading to higher customer satisfaction and loyalty. Similarly, AI-powered systems can automatically manage inventory levels, replenishing stock when necessary and optimizing supply chain management. By reducing the need for manual intervention, businesses can operate more efficiently and reduce costs, ultimately contributing to higher profit margins.

AI can greatly enhance the effectiveness of marketing and sales efforts, ultimately multiplying business results. AI algorithms can analyze customer behaviors, preferences, and purchasing patterns to create personalized marketing campaigns. By tailoring marketing messages to specific customer segments, businesses can increase the likelihood of generating favorable responses and conversions. This level of personalization not only enhances the customer experience but also improves marketing efficiency by preventing resources from being wasted on irrelevant audiences. AI can assist in lead generation and prospect identification. By utilizing machine learning algorithms, businesses can analyze vast amounts of data to identify potential customers who are most likely to convert. This targeted approach not only improves the efficiency of sales efforts but also increases the likelihood of closing deals, leading to higher revenue generation.

AI-powered analytics can greatly improve decision-making processes, enabling businesses to respond swiftly and appropriately to changing market conditions. By analyzing real-time data, AI algorithms can provide businesses with accurate and up-to-date insights, allowing them to make informed decisions promptly. Whether it be adjusting pricing strategies, reallocating marketing budgets, or developing new product offerings, AI can provide the necessary guidance to ensure effective decision-making. AI can generate accurate demand forecasts, enabling businesses to optimize inventory levels, minimize stockouts, and prevent overstocking. By aligning supply with demand, businesses can reduce costs associated with excess inventory or missed sales opportunities, contributing to increased profitability. AI can analyze market trends and competitor data to identify emerging opportunities or potential threats. Armed with this knowledge, businesses can adapt their strategies and stay ahead of the competition, ultimately multiplying business results. AI has the potential to greatly multiply business results through various applications. By collecting and analyzing vast amounts of data, AI enables businesses to gain valuable insights and make informed decisions more efficiently. AI-driven automation tools can streamline repetitive tasks, freeing up valuable time and resources. AI improves marketing and sales efforts by personalizing campaigns, enhancing customer experiences, and increasing the likelihood of conversions. AI-powered analytics greatly enhance decision-making processes, allowing businesses to respond swiftly to changing market conditions. With its versatility and ability to enhance business outcomes, AI truly has the potential to revolutionize the way businesses operate and multiply their results.

VI. CONCLUSION

The potential of AI in multiplying business results is undeniable. Throughout this essay, we have explored various ways in which AI can be leveraged to optimize different aspects of a business. From customer service to marketing and supply chain management, AI has the capability to revolutionize the way businesses operate and drive growth. By automating mundane tasks, enhancing decision-making processes, and improving overall efficiency, AI can free up valuable time and resources for businesses to focus on strategic initiatives and innovation. AI-powered analytics and predictive algorithms can provide invaluable insights into consumer behavior and market trends, enabling businesses to make data-driven decisions and stay ahead of their competition. It is important to acknowledge that the successful implementation of AI requires careful planning and consideration. Businesses must invest in the necessary infrastructure, data collection, and processing capabilities to fully harness the power of AI. Concerns surrounding ethical considerations, privacy, and security must be addressed to ensure the responsible use of AI technologies. Despite these challenges, the potential benefits of AI for businesses are immense. By embracing AI and incorporating it into their operations, companies can gain a competitive edge, achieve higher levels of productivity and efficiency, and ultimately, multiply their business results. As AI continues to advance and mature, it is expected that its impact on businesses will only grow stronger. It is crucial for businesses to start exploring and identifying opportunities to integrate AI into their strategies and adopt a proactive approach towards AI adoption. In today's rapidly evolving digital landscape, AI has become a necessity rather than a luxury. The businesses that fail to adapt and leverage the power of AI risk falling behind and losing their competitive advantage. It is imperative for businesses to recognize the potential of AI and take proactive measures to embrace this transformative technology. Whether it is through chatbots, machine learning algorithms, or predictive analytics, AI has the potential to transform the way businesses operate and amplify their results. The time to seize this opportunity is now. By embracing AI and leveraging its capabilities to streamline operations, enhance customer experiences, and drive innovation, businesses can position themselves for success in the digital age. With the right strategy and implementation, AI can propel businesses to new heights and open up a world of possibilities. It is important to approach AI adoption with caution and ensure that ethical and privacy concerns are addressed. By doing so, businesses can harness the full potential of AI while upholding their responsibility to society. AI is not merely a buzzword or a passing trend, but a game-changer that has the potential to revolutionize the business landscape. The businesses that embrace AI and leverage its capabilities will be the ones that thrive in the digital age. As technology continues to advance at a rapid pace, AI will undoubtedly play an increasingly pivotal role in shaping the future of businesses. It is imperative for businesses to invest in AI research and development, adopt a proactive approach towards AI adoption, and ensure that they have the right infrastructure and resources in place to capitalize on the immense power of this transformative technology. In doing so, businesses can multiply their results and gain a competitive edge in an increasingly crowded marketplace. The future belongs to those who have the courage to embrace change and leverage the power of AI. Will your business rise to the challenge?

SUMMARY OF THE MAIN POINTS DISCUSSED IN THE ESSAY

This essay discusses various ways in which businesses can effectively multiply their results by incorporating artificial intelligence (AI) into their operations. The first main point highlighted is the utilization of AI-driven customer relationship management (CRM) systems, which can enhance customer engagement and lead to improved sales conversion rates. By analyzing customer data, AI can provide valuable insights and personalize interactions, leading to greater customer satisfaction and loyalty. Secondly, the use of AI algorithms for predictive analytics is discussed as a means of identifying trends and patterns to optimize business strategies. Through AI, businesses can leverage real-time data to make informed decisions, anticipate customer needs, and adapt their offerings accordingly. The essay emphasizes the role of AI in streamlining business processes and enhancing operational efficiency. Automated workflows, powered by AI, can handle routine tasks, allowing employees to focus on more strategic activities. The integration of AI in supply chain management is highlighted as a way to optimize inventory levels, reduce costs, and improve delivery schedules. By forecasting demand and monitoring variables affecting the supply chain, AI enables better decisions and a more agile and responsive approach to inventory management. Another important point discussed is the use of AI-powered chatbots and virtual assistants in customer service. These tools can efficiently handle customer inquiries, provide instant responses, and offer personalized solutions, reducing human intervention and enhancing customer experiences. The essay emphasizes the growing role of AI in data security and fraud prevention. AI algorithms can detect anomalies and patterns, identifying potential threats or fraudulent activities more effectively than traditional methods. This contributes to safeguarding business operations and protecting sensitive customer information. The essay explores the emerging field of AI-driven content creation and marketing. By analyzing customer behavior and preferences, AI can generate personalized content and targeted marketing campaigns that resonate with the intended audience, thereby increasing conversion rates and brand engagement. The essay delves into the ethical considerations surrounding AI integration in business. It raises important questions related to data privacy, algorithm biases, and potential job displacement due to automation. The need for businesses to implement responsible AI practices, prioritize transparency, and engage in ongoing monitoring and evaluation to ensure fair and ethical use of AI is emphasized. Incorporating AI into businesses has the potential to significantly multiply results across various aspects, including customer engagement, predictive analytics, operational efficiency, supply chain management, customer service, data security, content creation, and marketing. It is crucial for businesses to approach AI integration with an ethical mindset, prioritizing the well-being of their employees and customers while ensuring responsible use of AI technology. By striking a balance between innovation and ethics, businesses can harness the power of AI to drive growth, improve customer experiences, and gain a competitive advantage in today's rapidly evolving business landscape.

THE POTENTIAL OF AI TO MULTIPLY BUSINESS RESULTS

The potential of artificial intelligence (AI) to multiply business results cannot be overemphasized. As discussed in the previous sections, AI technologies such as machine learning and natural language processing have proven to be instrumental in improving various business functions, including customer service, marketing, and operations. The ability of AI systems to analyze vast amounts of data and derive actionable insights enables businesses to make more informed decisions and respond quickly to market demands. AI-powered chatbots and virtual assistants enhance customer engagement by providing personalized and efficient support, thus improving customer satisfaction and loyalty. AI algorithms can optimize marketing campaigns by segmenting customers and targeting them with relevant and timely offers, leading to higher conversion rates and increased revenues. In the realm of operations, AI technologies can streamline processes, automate repetitive tasks, and enhance production efficiency, resulting in cost savings and improved productivity.

One of the key advantages of AI in the business realm is its ability to predict and adapt to future trends. AI algorithms can analyze historical data and identify patterns, enabling businesses to make accurate forecasts and predictions. This predictive capability is particularly valuable in industries that are prone to rapid changes and fluctuating market conditions. For example, in the retail industry, AI can analyze consumer behavior and purchasing patterns to predict future trends and optimize inventory management. By accurately anticipating demand, businesses can minimize stockouts and overstocks, thereby reducing costs and improving customer satisfaction. Similarly, in the financial sector, AI algorithms can monitor market trends, identify potential risks, and make data-driven investment decisions. This not only enhances profitability but also mitigates the risk of financial losses. AI has the potential to revolutionize decision-making processes within businesses. Traditional decision-making often relies on human intuition and experience, which can be subjective and biased. AI algorithms, on the other hand, are objective and data-driven, ensuring more accurate and unbiased decision-making. For instance, AI can analyze customer feedback and sentiment analysis to identify emerging issues or areas for improvement, enabling businesses to take proactive measures. AI systems can also provide recommendations and insights based on historical data, assisting managers in making informed decisions on pricing, product development, and resource allocation. By leveraging the power of AI, businesses can make strategic decisions that align with their goals and maximize their chances of success. The application of AI can lead to significant cost savings for businesses. By automating repetitive and time-consuming tasks, organizations can free up their human workforce to focus on more value-added activities. For example, in the healthcare industry, AI-powered medical imaging systems can analyze scans and identify anomalies, enabling radiologists to prioritize high-risk cases and improving diagnostic accuracy. Similarly, in the manufacturing sector, AI can be used for predictive maintenance, detecting potential equipment failures before they occur and preventing costly downtime. By reducing manual intervention and improving operational efficiency, businesses can achieve substantial cost savings and improve their bottom line. AI can help businesses enhance their competitive advantage in the marketplace. In today's fast-paced and digitally-driven world, organizations need to be agile and adaptive to stay ahead of the competition. AI technologies enable businesses to gain insights into their customers' preferences and behavior, allowing them to deliver personalized and targeted experiences. By understanding customers better, businesses can develop more effective marketing strategies, build stronger relationships, and win customer loyalty. AI can empower businesses to streamline their supply chains, optimize logistics, and improve overall operational efficiency. This not only reduces costs but also enables businesses to offer faster and more reliable services, gaining a competitive edge in the market.

The potential of AI to multiply business results is enormous. From improving customer service and marketing effectiveness to enhancing operational efficiency and decision-making, AI technologies have transformative power across various business functions. By leveraging AI capabilities, businesses can gain valuable insights, make accurate predictions, automate processes, and reduce costs, ultimately leading to increased profitability and competitiveness. As AI continues to evolve and mature, businesses that embrace this technology and leverage its potential strategically are likely to thrive in the ever-changing marketplace.

BUSINESSES SHOULD EMBRACE AI TECHNOLOGIES TO STAY COMPETITIVE AND ACHIEVE EXPONENTIAL GROWTH

As technology continues to advance at an unprecedented rate, businesses must adapt and evolve to remain competitive in today's fast-paced global economy. Artificial Intelligence (AI) is rapidly transforming various sectors, leading to enhanced efficiency, improved decision-making, and increased productivity. It is essential for businesses to embrace AI technologies in order to stay ahead in the race and achieve exponential growth.

One of the key reasons why businesses should adopt AI is to enhance their operational efficiency. AI-powered automation can streamline repetitive tasks, automate workflows, and reduce human error. By incorporating AI technologies, businesses can free up human resources to focus on higher-value activities, such as innovation, creativity, and strategic planning. This not only leads to cost savings but also enables employees to utilize their skills and expertise effectively, resulting in increased productivity and overall operational efficiency. AI can greatly improve decision-making processes within a business. With the ability to analyze vast amounts of data, AI can extract meaningful insights and provide valuable recommendations. This empowers businesses to make informed decisions, identify emerging trends, and predict market behavior with greater accuracy. By harnessing the power of AI, businesses can gain a competitive edge by making data-driven decisions, mitigating risks, and capitalizing on new opportunities in a timely manner.

In addition to operational efficiency and decision-making, embracing AI technologies can also significantly enhance customer experience. AI-powered chatbots and virtual assistants can provide round-the-clock customer support, address queries, and resolve issues promptly, thereby improving customer satisfaction and loyalty. AI algorithms can personalize marketing campaigns and recommendations based on individual customer preferences, leading to higher engagement and conversion rates. By leveraging AI, businesses can deliver personalized experiences at scale, cater to customers' evolving expectations, and gain a competitive advantage in today's customer-centric market landscape. Another compelling reason for businesses to adopt AI technologies is to boost their cybersecurity efforts. With the increasing frequency and sophistication of cyber threats, businesses need to have robust security measures in place. AI-driven algorithms can detect and respond to potential security breaches in real-time, enabling businesses to proactively protect their systems and data. By leveraging AI in cybersecurity, businesses can effectively minimize risks, safeguard sensitive information, and prevent financial loss or reputational damage.

Embracing AI technologies can open up new avenues for revenue growth and diversification. AI-powered analytics can identify untapped markets, consumer segments, and emerging products or services with high growth potential. By leveraging AI algorithms, businesses can develop targeted marketing strategies, optimize pricing strategies, and identify cross-selling or upselling opportunities. This enables businesses to expand their customer base, increase market share, and drive revenue growth.

AI technologies can also facilitate product innovation and development. By analyzing customer feedback, market trends, and competitor data, AI algorithms can identify gaps in the market and help businesses develop innovative products or services that cater to evolving customer needs. AI can enable businesses to carry out rapid prototyping, simulation, and testing, reducing time-to-market and minimizing costs associated with product development. By embracing AI, businesses can drive innovation, introduce disruptive products or services, and gain a competitive advantage in today's dynamic business landscape. Embracing AI technologies can contribute to a more sustainable and socially responsible business model. AI algorithms can optimize energy consumption, reduce waste, and minimize carbon footprints by optimizing processes and operations. AI can facilitate remote working and flexible schedules, contributing to a better work-life balance and reducing commuting-related emissions. By adopting AI, businesses can align their operations with sustainability goals, while also enhancing their brand reputation and attracting environmentally-conscious customers. Embracing AI technologies is no longer a choice but a necessity for businesses seeking to stay competitive and achieve exponential growth. By enhancing operational efficiency, improving decision-making processes, enhancing customer experience, bolstering cybersecurity efforts, diversifying revenue streams, driving product innovation, and promoting sustainability, businesses can unlock numerous benefits offered by AI. Businesses should proactively embrace AI technologies to thrive in today's rapidly evolving business landscape.

BIBLIOGRAPHY

Jaime Wood. 'The Word on College Reading and Writing.' Carol Burnell, Open Oregon Educational Resources, 1/1/2020

Bernd Carsten Stahl. 'Artificial Intelligence for a Better Future.' An Ecosystem Perspective on the Ethics of AI and Emerging Digital Technologies, Springer Nature, 3/17/2021

Murat Durmus. 'Machine Learning Pitfalls: A Brief Guide on How to Avoid Common Pitfalls (With Code Samples).' Murat Durmus, 3/12/2023

Woodrow Barfield. 'The Cambridge Handbook of the Law of Algorithms.' Cambridge University Press, 11/5/2020

Naveen Chilamkurti. 'The Adoption and Effect of Artificial Intelligence on Human Resources Management.' Pallavi Tyagi, Emerald Group Publishing, 2/10/2023

Julia Werner. 'Artificial Intelligence in Human Resource Management. Opportunities for the Aviation Industry.' GRIN Verlag, 7/19/2021

Darren G. Burton. 'AI Acceleration: A Comprehensive Guide to Adopting Artificial Intelligence in Your Business.' Darren G. Burton, 6/28/2023

Quigley, Marian. 'Encyclopedia of Information Ethics and Security.' Idea Group Inc (IGI), 5/31/2007

Committee on Regional Health Data Networks. 'Health Data in the Information Age.' Use, Disclosure, and Privacy, Institute of Medicine, National Academies Press, 1/1/1994

S. L. Aarthy. 'Integrating Deep Learning Algorithms to Overcome Challenges in Big Data Analytics.' R. Sujatha, CRC Press, 9/22/2021

Martha Rogers. 'Managing Customer Experience and Relationships.' A Strategic Framework, Don Peppers, John Wiley & Sons, 4/26/2022

Sara Quach. 'Artificial Intelligence for Marketing Management.' Park Thaichon, Taylor & Francis, 11/10/2022

Gerhard Friedrich. 'Information and Management Systems for Product Customization.' Thorsten Blecker, Springer Science & Business Media, 12/28/2005

Karthik Ramasubramanian. 'Building an Enterprise Chatbot.' Work with Protected Enterprise Data Using Open Source Frameworks, Abhishek Singh, Apress, 9/13/2019

Mayfair Digital Agency. 'Chatbots and AI Assistants Transforming Customer Support.' Mayfair Digital Agency, 3/6/2020

Mayfair Digital Agency. 'AI-Powered Chatbots: Enhancing Customer Service and Sales.' Mayfair Digital Agency, 3/4/2021

Nick Toman. 'The Effortless Experience.' Conquering the New Battleground for Customer Loyalty, Matthew Dixon, Penguin, 9/12/2013

Minghai Zheng. 'AI-Based Personalization.' Transforming Relationships Between Companies and Customers, Amazon Digital Services LLC - Kdp, 6/2/2023

Alan Pennington. 'The Customer Experience Manual.' How to design, measure and improve customer experience in your business, Pearson UK, 9/14/2016

Robert J. Zwerling. 'AI-Enabled Analytics for Business.' A Roadmap for Becoming an Analytics Powerhouse, Lawrence S. Maisel, John Wiley & Sons, 1/19/2022

Tanupriya Choudhury. 'Decision Intelligence Analytics and the Implementation of Strategic Business Management.' P. Mary Jeyanthi, Springer Nature, 1/1/2022

Emily Flynn Vencat. 'Custom Nation.' Why Customization Is the Future of Business and How to Profit From It, Anthony Flynn, BenBella Books, Inc., 11/15/2012

Frank Kane. 'Building Recommender Systems with Machine Learning and AI.' Help People Discover New Products and Content with Deep Learning, Neural Networks, and Machine Learning Recommendations., Independently Published, 8/11/2018

Tom Fawcett. 'Data Science for Business.' What You Need to Know about Data Mining and Data-Analytic Thinking, Foster Provost, "O'Reilly Media, Inc.", 7/27/2013

Division on Engineering and Physical Sciences. 'Massive Data Sets.' Proceedings of a Workshop, National Research Council, National Academies Press, 2/10/1997

Minghai Zheng. 'AI for Decision Making.' Leveraging Machine Learning to Make Better Choices, Amazon Digital Services LLC - Kdp, 5/29/2023

Kaveh Memarzadeh. 'Artificial Intelligence in Healthcare.' Adam Bohr, Academic Press, 6/21/2020

Thomas H. Davenport. 'Artificial Intelligence.' The Insights You Need from Harvard Business Review, Harvard Business Review, Harvard Business Review Press, 1/1/2019

Joshua Walker. 'Outsmarting AI.' Power, Profit, and Leadership in the Age of Machines, Brennan Pursell, Rowman & Littlefield, 8/15/2020

Ciara Heavin. 'Decision Support, Analytics, and Business Intelligence, Third Edition.' Daniel J. Power, Business Expert Press, 6/8/2017

Nicolas Vandeput. 'Data Science for Supply Chain Forecasting.' Walter de Gruyter GmbH & Co KG, 3/22/2021

Amir Ali Shaik. 'Mastering Operations in the Corporate World.' Amir Ali Shaik, 6/27/2023

Sanjana Mohapatra. 'Process Automation Strategy in Services, Manufacturing and Construction.' Bharati Mohapatra, Emerald Group Publishing, 2/20/2023

Bernard Marr. 'Artificial Intelligence in Practice.' How 50 Successful Companies Used AI and Machine Learning to Solve Problems, John Wiley & Sons, 4/15/2019

David Vivancos. 'Automate Or Be Automated.' Independently Published, 3/27/2020

Gwynne Richards. 'Warehouse Management.' A Complete Guide to Improving Efficiency and Minimizing Costs in the Modern Warehouse, Kogan Page Publishers, 6/3/2014

Dwayne Anderson. 'Artificial Intelligence Implementing AI for your Business.' Estalontech, 9/26/2021